Redeemed & Restored

The Stories of Twelve Ordinary Women
Transformed by God's Extraordinary Power

CALVARY CHAPEL PASTORS' WIVES

Redeemed & Restored

The Stories of Twelve Ordinary Women Transformed by God's Extraordinary Power

COMPILED BY JUNE HESTERLY & SANDY MACINTOSH

CALVARY CHAPEL
PUBLISHING

Redeemed and Restored: The Stories of Twelve Ordinary Women Transformed by God's Extraordinary Power

Copyright © 2006 by June Hesterly and Sandy MacIntosh

Published by Calvary Chapel Publishing (CCP),
A resource ministry of Calvary Chapel of Costa Mesa
3800 South Fairview Road
Santa Ana, California 92704

First printing, 2005
Second printing, 2006

All Scripture quotations in this book, unless otherwise indicated, are taken from the New King James Version. Copyright © 1982, Thomas Nelson, Inc. Used by permission. All rights reserved.

Scriptures marked (KJV) are taken from the King James Version.

Scripture quotations marked (NIV) are taken from the HOLY BIBLE, NEW INTERNATIONAL VERSION®. NIV®. Copyright © 1973, 1978, 1984 by International Bible Society. Used by permission of Zondervan. All rights reserved.

Cover layout and design by Aric Everson.
Inside page layout and design by Lakeside Design Plus.

ISBN 10 1-59751-019-X
ISBN 13 978-1-59751-019-6

Printed in the United States of America.

Dedication

We, the redeemed and restored women of this book, lovingly dedicate these stories to our wonderful husbands:

Chuck Smith
Bob Coy
Bil Gallatin
Skip Heitzig
Jim Hesterly
Jeff Johnson
Greg Laurie
Mike MacIntosh
Steve Mays
Don McClure
Raul Ries
Malcolm Wild

TO GOD BE THE GLORY

Acknowledgments

We would like to thank everyone at Calvary Chapel Publishing and Calvary Distribution for their support, especially Lance Emma and Ed Cornwell, whose commitment to this project made it happen; Katie Ayub, whose administrative gift kept us on track; and Gayle Stacy, for her last-minute transcription work. We would also like to thank Romy Godding for her meticulous proofreading, Aric Everson for his beautiful cover design, and Barb and Dan Malda for the dynamic page layout. A special thank you to Christine Scheller; her sweet and tender editing has brought life and light to all of our words and thoughts, and her love for God and for this book has inspired us all.

Contents

Introduction

These are the stories and testimonies of ordinary pastors' wives whose lives have been redeemed and restored by an extraordinary God and His extraordinary love. It is our hope and prayer that you, the reader, will be reminded of your own story of redemption and be encouraged to press on and live a life that honors God and speaks of His wonderful grace.

I press toward the goal for the prize
of the upward call of God in Christ Jesus.
Philippians 3:14

Kay Smith

Pleasing to God

By Janette Manderson

"I do always those things that please him."
John 8:29, KJV

It was a warm day in Los Angeles, California, when a young mother appeared at the door of the Johnson house with her tiny baby girl in her arms. She said she wanted to leave her baby to be looked after by Mrs. Johnson while she and her husband went through a divorce. She said her name was Helen Wood and that her baby was named Catherine Wood.

Mrs. Johnson was a registered nurse who took babies into her home to care for them while the baby's custody was being decided in divorce court. She had started this ministry the year before when she and her husband, Oscar, became Christians.

Minnie Ethel O'Judy Williamson was a pretty widow with a married daughter when she met Oscar Johnson. Oscar had an executive position with an oil company. He was soft-spoken, intelligent, and gentle. Minnie was charming, charismatic, and temperamental. She was a vibrant woman who had married very young and had her first baby, Louise, at the age of sixteen. She was widowed at the age of twenty-four and moved to Arizona to start a restaurant in a mining camp to support her daughter. Determined to protect herself and her daughter, she even carried a gun!

When Minnie's daughter was sixteen years old, they moved to Kansas and went to nursing school, earning degrees as registered nurses. Soon after graduation, Louise married and moved away. It was at this time that Minnie met the much-younger Oscar.

Oscar fell in love with the captivating Minnie and they were married. Minnie created a home where Oscar was treated with respect. When he came home from work, anyone sitting in "his chair" would have to get up and let Oscar sit down. Minnie didn't allow him to get up from the dining room table to get anything either. Minnie would lovingly wait on him. Oscar was also extremely loving to his wife, buying a beautiful home for her in the Silver Lake area of Los Angeles, California, and allowing her to furnish and decorate it to her taste. He even fixed breakfast for her every morning.

In September 1926 Louise became a Christian and led her mother and stepfather to the Lord. This was a turning point in their lives. Louise began attending LIFE Bible College in Los Angeles. Minnie wanted a ministry, so she decided to open her home to babies whose custody was being decided in the courts. She thought, *Oh, what an opportunity to pray over these babies and little children!* Louise and others helped to care for the babies. When baby Catherine was placed in the home, Louise liked her best. She said that her mother and the other attendants liked the fat, happy babies, but Louise loved fussy, tiny Catherine. Louise and the baby soon bonded, and they loved each other dearly.

Helen Wood never returned for her baby girl. She wrote letters and sent money and beautiful clothes for her baby, but she did not provide her address. Once, when Catherine was a little girl, she called to ask about visiting her. Minnie did not want little Catherine to be upset or confused, so she refused the visit. When the Johnsons realized that Catherine's mother wasn't going to reclaim her, they knew that God had given them a baby to raise as their own daughter. They named her Catheryn Louise Johnson (changing the spelling of her first name to honor a friend) and kept her adoption a secret from her.

Catheryn grew up in comfortable circumstances in Los Angeles. A sensitive, intelligent girl, she was closer to her gentle daddy than to her more outspoken mother. When Catheryn would bring work home from school, Oscar always took time to look at it and appreciate it. If he didn't think she did something especially well, he would say, "Catheryn, this is very good, but you can do better." Oscar spoke to his daughter with so much love that Catheryn always wanted to please him. On the other hand, Minnie's perfectionist tendencies (she would rewrap Christmas gifts in blue and silver paper so that all the gifts under the tree would match) and uncertain temper made the shy, studious Catheryn afraid of displeasing her.

Minnie loved Catheryn and felt that it was her duty to train her socially. She forced Catheryn out of her introverted behavior and helped her to compensate by developing a sparkling wit and excellent manners. Minnie bought her beautiful clothes for church and took her to the beauty salon to have her hair done every week. She didn't think it was important for Catheryn to have beautiful clothes for school, however. In fifth and sixth grades, when the other girls were wearing bobby socks, Catheryn was wearing long, black, cotton bloomers and heavy, black cotton hose—items her mother felt were appropriate for little girls to wear to school. Catheryn felt miserable and embarrassed, but she still managed to make many friends and even joined the flag twirling team in junior high.

Minnie wanted Catheryn to play musical instruments, so she arranged for her to have piano and clarinet lessons. Catheryn was in the Silver Band, along with her parents, at Angelus Temple in Los Angeles, where her family attended church.

Catheryn began to go by the nickname, Kay, which she thought was more sophisticated, when she was in high school. Though Minnie disliked the name, Kay was beginning to think for herself. She sneaked more fashionable clothes to school (her mother disapproved of the current fashions in the 1940s), and even wore lipstick when she was out, carefully wiping it off before returning home.

World War II was affecting all of America and Kay's parents bought a ranch in Hemet, California, to grow chickens and vegetables so the family could provide food for themselves and leave more for the war effort. Minnie's relatives took care of the ranch during the week, and Kay went there with her parents each weekend. At first they would drive to Hemet on Saturday morning and return Saturday night so they would be back in time for church on Sunday. Then they started going on Friday night, and eventually began returning Sunday evening. Though Kay enjoyed the ranch and the horse her parents kept there for her, she was sad that they had stopped attending church on Sundays. Gradually, her parents slipped into behavior that they had formerly believed was sinful.

Kay was filled with questions and conflicting emotions as she watched her parents growing cold spiritually. It was about this time that Kay learned that she had been adopted. A young relative blurted out the information and Kay went to her mother for confirmation of what she had heard. Minnie told Kay the story of her birth mother and even read aloud the letters that her birth mother had written to Minnie. It was heart-wrenching for Kay, especially as she watched Minnie tear up the letters after she had read them.

One night on the way to Hemet, Kay and her parents were involved in a serious car accident. The occupants of the other car were killed. Kay was bruised but unhurt. Her parents, shaken by the accident, stopped their weekly trips to the ranch. Soon afterward Minnie suffered a debilitating stroke. She was bedridden and required constant nursing, so Minnie's sister moved into the family's home to help with Minnie's care, disrupting the family relationships that had been so strong.

Kay began to feel like an outsider in her own home. Her mother was ill and her father was despondent. Kay reacted like many teenagers would have: she rebelled. She was eighteen years old and in college, so she began to make choices that she knew would displease her parents—if they only knew. The secular humanism and contempt for the things of God expressed by her professors reinforced her pain and disillusionment. She thought, *They're right; there's nothing to the Christian faith*, and decided that she didn't believe in God at all. She made good grades and behaved well at home, so her parents were unaware that she was slipping away from the things she had learned about God when she was in church.

When Kay was twenty years old, her sister Louise visited from Arizona, where she was now a pastor in the International Church of the Foursquare Gospel denomination. She had always adored Kay and was an astute judge of character. She quickly realized that Kay was leading a double life and was in danger spiritually. Louise talked Minnie into allowing Kay to go to summer camp with a church group. It was there that Kay gave her heart back to the Lord and rededicated her life to Him. She went home and broke her engagement to the unsaved young man she still loved, left her secular college, and enrolled in LIFE Bible College.

The following spring, in April 1948, Kay went to a LIFE baseball game. She wore a white dress and piled her dark hair on top of her head, accenting the style with a white gardenia. When twenty-year-old Chuck Smith saw her arrive at the game, he asked a mutual friend to introduce them and quickly brushed off the seat next to him so Kay would sit there. (On their twenty-fifth wedding anniversary, Chuck bought Kay a gardenia plant and planted it right outside their kitchen window to commemorate this day. It blooms in June, the month they were married.)

Soon, they were dating as often as possible. Kay realized that Chuck was different from the other young men she had dated. He was more mature and he loved to talk about the Lord and about the Bible. She also loved his family. She could see that they were sincere Christians who lived for God. Chuck's mom, Maude Elizabeth, was very kind and welcoming and made Kay feel at home; his married older sister, Virginia, was friendly and warm; his two younger brothers were funny and liked to tease her; and his dad was the perfect gentleman, with courtly manners.

When Chuck and Kay were dating, Kay's dad had a funny little routine to let them know when it was time for Chuck to go home. Chuck and Kay would be visiting in the front room of the house after Oscar and Minnie had gone to bed. Suddenly, they would hear a slipper hit the floor. That would be the first sign that it was time for Chuck to leave. Sign number two was when they heard footsteps in her parents' bedroom, and sign number three was Oscar appearing at the door and saying, "Catheryn, don't you think you'd better let that young man go home?" Catheryn never wanted the young man to go home, but it was a wonderful protection, and Chuck would later do similar things when his own daughters were dating.

Chuck had graduated from LIFE Bible College the year they met and he was guest speaking at various churches while he waited to be appointed to his own church. He would tell Kay about the sermons he was planning to preach while they went sailing or went to the beach. On June 19, 1948, Chuck and Kay were married in a small, private ceremony in the home of one of their favorite pastors. Since Kay's mother was too ill to plan a formal wedding, and because Chuck and Kay wanted to get into full-time ministry as soon as possible, they felt that a small family wedding was best. After their honeymoon, the newlyweds were assigned to their first church in Prescott, Arizona. Chuck earned the modest sum of fifteen-dollars-a-month, so Kay looked for work. Her style and clothes from Los Angeles were unusual and sophisticated in small-town Prescott. The mayor hired Kay as his secretary.

A few months later, Kay realized that the "flu" she had been experiencing was actually morning sickness and that a baby was on the way. Chuck was thrilled and declared that the baby had to be a girl. One day the Smiths went on a hospital call to the only hospital in the area. It was not at all modern and they were alarmed at the idea of their baby being born there, so they resigned from the Prescott church and moved back to California. For the next few months, Chuck and Kay awaited the baby's birth at Chuck's parents' house; and finally, on April 19, 1949, Janette Lynn Smith was born. Three weeks later, the Smiths moved to Tucson, Arizona, where Chuck would pastor their second church.

In Tucson the church provided living quarters for the young family. There was a large, rectangular room at the back of the church with a concrete floor. On one end of the room, there was a faucet protruding from the wall, which provided cold water. They had to heat the water on the stove to wash their dishes. Next to the faucet were a stove and a refrigerator that a church member had donated. That was the kitchen. They used drapes to divide the room into sections, so they had a living room with a dining area and a bedroom. Someone gave Chuck and Kay furniture made of mohair, which was so coarse that Kay had to cover it with sheets before they could sit on it. The only bathrooms were on the other side of the church.

Kay was a "city girl" who was unaccustomed to such primitive conditions. This was the school in which she learned, as a young pastor's wife, to pray and depend upon the Lord for all her needs. Kay and Chuck were young and energetic; the living space was a challenge they accepted, and they soon created a cozy little home out of the space.

On her very first Sunday as a pastor's wife, a woman walked up to Kay after church, handed her a Sunday school quarterly, and said, "Now that you're here, you can take over my class." Kay was terrified. She thought, *What if someone asks me a question that I can't answer?* Even though she had been to Bible college, she wasn't confident that she understood the Bible well enough to teach it. Chuck advised her to get a *Halley's Bible Handbook.* She carried that reference book with her to church every Sunday for several years. If someone asked her a question she couldn't answer, Kay would open her *Halley's Bible Handbook* and find an answer.

God blessed the church in Tucson and it was soon growing. Young people from the nearby University of Arizona began to attend, and Chuck and Kay would take a group out street-witnessing on Saturday nights. Kay played a little pump organ at services in the park twice a week (sometimes the temperature was one-hundred-and-ten degrees) and visited the sick twice a week. She and Chuck started an around-the-clock prayer chain. They prayed finances into the church because the people were so poor—many of them didn't even have indoor plumbing. They also prayed people into the church, and sometimes had to pray them out! A false teacher once told Chuck, "I'm going to see you in your coffin if you don't start preaching this doctrine." Chuck and Kay were in their early twenties when they faced this challenge, but God protected Chuck, and instead of any harm coming to him, the false teacher died of a brain tumor two weeks later.

God often supernaturally provided for Chuck and Kay during this time. Chuck was paid on Mondays and they usually ran out of money by Thursday. One Saturday night when Kay was pregnant with their second child, they were trying to figure out how they were going to make it until Monday. Kay was scrubbing the parsonage when someone knocked on the back door. Chuck opened the door to find a beautiful man and woman who looked as if they had just stepped out of *Vogue* or *Bazaar*. They wanted to get married. The church janitor agreed to be a witness, but they needed another one, so Kay reluctantly came out from where she was hiding. She was mortified because she was wearing an old, blue polka-dot dress. As the newlyweds left, the man shook Chuck's hand and gave him a one hundred dollar bill! Kay learned faith through these kinds of experiences.

When Kay was eight months pregnant, a couple in the church asked the Smiths to house-sit for six months. The young family moved into a brand-new, two-bedroom house that was fully carpeted. It even had a record player! Every morning Chuck would play records and they would praise God for such a lovely home. But when Kay had moved out of the little parsonage behind the church, she cried. She had grown to love their little shelter where she and Chuck had seen many people come to Christ and where they had created a happy home.

The next month, when Kay was nine months pregnant, she received a call with terrible news: her father—gentle, loving Oscar—was dead from a heart attack. He was only fifty-three years old. Against doctor's orders (Kay was due to deliver her baby at any time), they made the long, sad drive home to Los Angeles for the funeral. Kay's "perfect daddy" was in heaven and she would miss him all her life.

Charles Ward Smith Junior was born later that month on June 28, 1951. Chuck had said that this baby would be a boy and baby Chuck was a darling baby boy with beautiful, blue eyes and dark, soft hair who was a comfort to Kay as she grieved for her daddy. She nicknamed the baby "Chuckles."

A year later Chuck was offered a church in Corona, California. He eagerly accepted the challenge of taking a tiny church and helping it to grow. They found a house to rent and made room for one more, as adorable baby, Jeffrey Wayne Smith, joined the family on March 27, 1953. Jeffrey was a happy, easygoing baby, and it was a good thing, because the family was busy all the time. The church didn't grow as large or as fast as the one in Tucson had, so Chuck had to support the family by working in the local market to supplement his small salary from the church. There were mostly older people living in Corona at that time. Chuck and Kay missed the young couples who had been their friends in Arizona. It could have been a dry time spiritually, but God faithfully provided just the right circumstances to grow their faith and to prepare them for the future ministries He had for them.

Kay's mother, Minnie, was worried about how Kay was coping with three young children, ages four, two, and newborn. She wrote tender letters to Kay expressing her concern, but soon the concern was for Minnie, as she grew ill again. This time, she didn't recover and Kay was again attending a parent's funeral. Her sister was the only member left from her original family. They became closer than ever.

In 1954, when Kay was twenty-seven years old, a church in Huntington Beach, California, became available. Chuck was ready for a new challenge. There was even a parsonage next door with two bedrooms and one bathroom. The family moved in and enjoyed living on the church grounds. Kay loved to take the children to the brand-new public library across the street. Janette was in kindergarten and attended the reading program at the library while Kay browsed among the books.

It was a precious time for the Smith family. Chuck matured in his teaching ministry and in his understanding of what God wanted him to do about church growth. The concept of "sheep begetting sheep" was given to Chuck by God when Chuck realized that a healthy church would grow without all the contests and competitions that were popular in those days. Instead, the Lord would grow the church by leading the church members to share their faith with their families and friends. Chuck's job was to feed the flock and to nurture their growth so that they would be healthy spiritually.

Soon the church was filled with young families. Kay helped out as the Sunday school superintendent, the church pianist, and sometimes, as the worship leader. She wrote a Christmas play (starring Chuck, of course) that was very well received, and she also organized the children in the church for Christmas and Easter programs that they would present to the congregation.

Chuck and Kay rarely had a chance to talk before services on Sunday mornings, so when Chuck would walk to the pulpit to preach, he would always pass Kay sitting at the piano, put his hand on her shoulder, and give it a squeeze—letting her know that, even in the midst of ministry, he was thinking of her.

A difficult time came in November 1957, when Chuck's younger brother, Bill, and Chuck's dad, Charles, were killed in a plane that Bill was flying. The plane crashed in Camp Pendleton as Bill was flying to Orange County from San Diego in a heavy windstorm. The news of their deaths was on the front page of the newspaper, and their funeral was crowded with people who knew Chuck's gregarious dad and young people who knew the popular Bill. Chuck managed to preach a strong salvation message to the large audience, though his heart was breaking over the deaths. Kay lost her voice from the pressure of holding back her tears.

On April 4, 1960, the family had a joyous occasion to celebrate when Cheryl Lynn Smith was born. Since the other kids were older, the whole family doted on this beautiful baby girl. Everyone enjoyed having a baby around the house again. Three weeks later it was time to move because Chuck had accepted a position at Los Serranos Community Church in Chino, California. This church also had a parsonage on the grounds, so Kay settled the family into the house while Chuck started meeting the church members.

These were busy days for Kay. The church was much bigger than the one in Huntington Beach. Kay didn't have a dryer or disposable diapers, so clean diapers were always hanging on the clothesline in the parsonage backyard. The phone rang off the hook with various needs from the people at church. If Chuck wasn't there, Kay was expected to provide help and counsel. Scriptures like Philippians 4:6, *Be anxious for nothing, but in everything by prayer and supplication, with thanksgiving, let your requests be made known to God,* strengthened Kay as God prepared her for the enormous work that lay ahead.

After three years, in June 1963, the Smiths moved again to what would be their last church in the Foursquare denomination. Chuck and Kay wanted a home of their own, so they found a house on a large lot around the corner from Newport Harbor High School in Newport Beach and moved in. Chuck's mom, his last link to the denomination, died the following year. Soon, Chuck felt called to leave the denomination and start an independent church.

He founded Corona Christian Center in Corona, California, and the family moved there in February 1965. The church was flourishing, the church members were wonderful, and the family was settling into life in Corona when Chuck received a call from a small, independent church in Costa Mesa. The church was called Calvary Chapel of Costa Mesa. When Chuck told Kay that he felt the Lord wanted him to take the pastorate of Calvary Chapel, Kay was very surprised. The family had moved to Corona less than a year before and the Corona church was growing every week. She was concerned about moving the children again and worried that the church members would be hurt. But Chuck was sure that God was calling him to Costa Mesa.

Kay was able to see that God was doing something new, so the move back to the house in Newport Beach took place in February 1966. Kay started a morning prayer meeting with the women of the church while Cheryl attended kindergarten. She was in her late thirties then and most of the other women were older than sixty years. Kay thought they were the sweetest, dearest, godliest, most loving women she had ever met. Whenever they prayed together, she was lifted up in the Lord and left wanting to live a holier life. Week after week, the little group would pray, "Lord, give us men who will be soldiers of the cross. Set these men on high and make them the 'zingiest' Christians in the world." God answered their prayers and sent wonderfully gifted, born-again men to come alongside Chuck. (Kay has often said that the untold story of Calvary Chapel of Costa Mesa is that the church has always been saturated in prayer from its earliest days.)

Soon, the tiny church on Church Street was filled to overflowing and it was time to move. This time, the church moved and the Smiths stayed where they were! The new church was built on the lot of an old school, Greenville School, on the border of Costa Mesa and Santa Ana. The name Calvary Chapel of Costa Mesa was retained.

Janette, Chuck Junior, and Jeff were now in their teens, and Janette had a boyfriend named John. He had been a hippie but had given his heart to the Lord and was now attending a Christian college. John would talk to Kay about his hippie days because she was intrigued by the hippies who were filling the beaches of Southern California. She would sometimes cry because she felt their emptiness so deeply. It was as if she would rather die than have them go on without Christ.

One day Janette was late getting ready when John came to pick her up, and Kay finally had a chance to talk to him at length. She wanted to know everything there was to know about hippies: what they believed, what kind of homes they came from, what their experiences were. She said, "John, if you meet a hippie, bring him to our house so we can talk to him." John took her up on her offer and brought Lonnie Frisbee over to meet Kay. Lonnie had long hair and a beard, but he also had a Bible under his arm. He and his wife, Connie, stayed with the Smiths for about three weeks. Lonnie and Connie would go out and pick up kids and bring them to church. Soon, hippies were filling the church every night of the week, crowding in to hear Pastor Chuck, Lonnie Frisbee, and the various bands that performed.

While Janette, Chuck Junior, and Jeff were happy to go to Calvary most nights of the week, Kay went two nights a week and stayed home the other nights to get little Cheryl into bed. Kay made a conscious decision to be faithful to her ministry as a mother while she still had a little one at home who needed her mommy to tuck her in. Her commitment to her family during these days of explosive growth at Calvary Chapel provided a solid foundation for the four children.

Kay was a fun-loving mother. Once when she was roller-skating with Cheryl and some other neighborhood children on the street in front of their house, a church board member arrived for a meeting. To avoid being seen, Kay skated right into the carpeted front room of their house! She also tried to make dinnertime special when the children were growing up. She would get a Bible quiz going and it would get very competitive. The kids would also take turns playing word games or trying to make up riddles, and the whole family would enjoy the attempts of Jeff or Cheryl as they tried to join in. Many of the family's "inside jokes" stem from funny things one of the kids said during those times.

Before long it was obvious that the church would have to move again. In 1973 Calvary Chapel moved in to the buildings at its present location at Fairview Road and Sunflower Avenue on the border of Costa Mesa and Santa Ana. Kay was asked to start a women's Bible study at Jean McClure's house about this time. (Jean's husband, Don, was an assistant pastor at Calvary Chapel.) It wasn't long before the house was too crowded, so the women began meeting in the church's fellowship hall. When the study outgrew the fellowship hall, it was moved into the main sanctuary, where it still meets on Friday mornings. The Lord gave the "Pleasing to God" messages to Kay during those early days. Later, her studies were developed into the Joyful Life classes that still meet today. By then Cheryl was grown up, and Kay felt that she could devote the time to writing lessons, studying for them, and presenting them each Friday without detriment to her youngest child.

Kay also created boards to plan for women's retreats that were held once in the fall and once in the spring. The retreat boards would prayerfully choose a theme and invite a speaker to come and share a message based on the theme. There would be visual aids in the form of centerpieces at the dining room tables and on the platform in the retreat meeting room to help reinforce the message of the theme. These retreats grew so popular that Calvary Chapel had to start holding two retreats each spring and fall.

Since several other Calvary Chapels had formed by this time, Kay was concerned that there were a lot of young pastors' wives who needed encouragement in their ministries. She knew from experience how difficult it could be to try to keep a family healthy physically and spiritually while supporting a husband in the work of the church. The pastors' wives conferences were started to minister to these women. The goal was (and still remains) to strengthen and equip Calvary Chapel pastors' wives for the unique work that God has given to them.

As the years have gone by, all four of Chuck and Kay's children have married and had families of their own. Janette has four children, Chuck Junior has five children, Jeff has six children, and Cheryl has four children. Now there are fourteen great-grandchildren to add to the joy when everyone gathers at Chuck and Kay's house for Christmas. They thank God every year as they gather, because Chuck and Kay like having their family close to them.

Kay is still active in the work at Calvary Chapel of Costa Mesa. Since Chuck didn't retire at age sixty-five and Kay wants to spend time with him, she goes to work with him each day. They are spending these years as they did when they married over fifty-seven years ago—serving God together in the ministry.

Biography

Popular women's speaker and author, Kay Smith, is director of the Joyful Life women's ministry at Calvary Chapel of Costa Mesa, where she has served alongside her husband of fifty-eight years, Chuck Smith. Chuck is the founder of Calvary Chapel, which has over 1,500 affiliates worldwide, along with numerous Bible colleges and conference centers.

Diane Coy

Second Chances

For we are God's workmanship, created in Christ Jesus to
do good works, which God prepared in advance for us to do.
Ephesians 2:19, NIV

One day when I was a junior in high school, I pleaded with my family, "Can we please go to church? I think we really need God." To my surprise, everyone agreed and we began attending a local church. Unfortunately, the church was kind of stuffy and we didn't seem to have the right clothes. Even though we wore bright fluorescent visitor tags, the people there completely ignored us. Afterward we would go out for Sunday brunch, which always included champagne.

It wasn't long before I began to develop the distinct impression that going to church was actually making our family situation worse than it had been before. We decided to stop going. Things got really bad for me after that. I felt that if God wasn't interested in helping us, then there was no good reason to include Him in my life. Like many troubled young people, the innocence and simple faith I had known as a child were being extinguished by pain, disillusionment, and sin.

I was born and raised in Hacienda Heights, California, the third of four children. I have two brothers and one sister. Religion was not part of our family life. I have a faded memory of my mom reading a book to me that talked about God creating everything, but other than that we never really talked about the Lord. I don't recall even having a Bible in our house.

There was a brief time, however, when my parents dropped us off at a Baptist church for Sunday school. It was great, but after a couple of weeks, a girl in my class mentioned "big people church." I asked, "What's big people church?" She said it was where the parents went while we were in Sunday school. I didn't understand because I thought Sunday school was like regular school—parents didn't go there just like they didn't go to school with us Monday through Friday.

I had a lot of confusing times growing up and some of them weren't as humorous as this one. Some of them were quite painful. I came from a very loving family; however, my family suffered with alcoholism and all the issues that surround that addiction.

I shared a room with my sister, Linda, the entire time I lived at home. She was four years older than me and I always looked up to her. She probably would have liked me to be more like her too because my side of the room was always a big mess and hers wasn't! We were quite different in many ways. She was the popular one, the confident one, the outgoing one. She was a model, a cheerleader, and a member of the high school homecoming court. She dated the star of the football team, which thrilled my dad to no end. I always compared myself to her. It wasn't her fault, but

I grew up in her shadow and always felt like I could never do enough or be good enough. I wasn't like Linda—at all.

This made high school a nightmare for me since I arrived there after my sister had made her debut. And everybody knew who Linda was. In fact my teachers would compare me to her. It must have been a real shock to them when I didn't make it onto the cheerleading squad. It wasn't to me. And I didn't like any of the football stars.

There were quite a few well-to-do kids at my high school and *Jordache* jeans could make or break a person socially. Unfortunately, *Jordache* jeans never fit me. I was shy and withdrawn and I felt like I was a failure and a disappointment to everyone, including myself. It wasn't long before I became really negative and decided not even to try anymore. I became a typical rebellious teenager, joining a group in our school that was basically the *Jordache* rejects. We had the mentality that life was about getting all the gusto we could get while we could get it. I started ditching school, which provided a lot of idle time for getting into things I shouldn't have gotten into. I began taking drugs and even sold them a couple of times. I also started drinking—a lot. It's no wonder that life became full of disappointment and rejection for me.

I found myself in constant pursuit of male attention. My relationships were so unhealthy that if I set my sight on a guy and he paid attention to me too quickly, I wasn't interested anymore. On the other hand, if he took too long to show interest, I would get disappointed and think, *Oh, I'm just not good enough. I knew it.* My life became one ongoing search for the next party and the next guy.

During my junior year in high school things in my family weren't going well. For this reason, I never wanted my friends to visit our home and I convinced my family that we needed to find God. When going to church didn't solve our problems, I began living day-by-day, trying to get attention. I wanted someone to stop me from doing the things I was doing; I wanted anyone to say, "You're worth more than this. There's more value to your life. You don't have to behave this way." Instead, every time I got into trouble I was given another chance.

In my junior year I was absent from school more often than I was present. I had a friend named Penny who would write notes to the principal for me that said things like, "Diane cannot attend school today due to an appointment with the podiatrist." We didn't even know what a podiatrist was, but that year I had many appointments with people like podiatrists. When I finally got called into the vice-principal's office, he was very concerned. He looked at my records and asked me where I had been. And then he said, "We should send you to vocational school, but we like you, so we're going to give you a second chance."

My life became a series of second chances. The wilder I became, the more second chances I seemed to get. I should have considered myself the luckiest lady on planet earth. But halfway through my senior year, at the age of eighteen, I became hopeless and actually began to think of suicide. I felt like I was destined to fail, and although I had a lot of boyfriends and friends, I was lonely all the time. A strange thing began to happen. My heart became hard toward people and I became very unapproachable. I got into new wave and punk rock music. I would wear trench coats and do my hair different styles. I was searching so hard for my own identity because I was totally unsatisfied with who I was.

Meanwhile my sister's football star boyfriend (who is now my brother-in-law whom I love) was going to school in San Diego. He was invited to the Calvary Chapel there (which is now Horizon Christian Fellowship), and he gave his heart to Jesus. While my sister was visiting him, she went to church with him and she also gave her heart to the Lord. She called to tell me, and when she got back she found a Calvary Chapel in West Covina, California, that was right near our house. She loved the senior pastor, Raul Ries, and started going all the time.

This didn't really have the impact on me that it should have had because I figured my sister was a "good person" who belonged in church. It made sense to me. What also made sense was that I was a "bad person" who didn't belong in church. So when she would invite me to go with her, I would think, *Nah, you belong there. I don't.* I didn't take her up on her invitation for a long time.

But then people started getting born again at my high school. They weren't all "good people" like Linda. They were people like me. A girl named Kim, who I knew really well, was the envy of all our friends because her parents grew pot in their backyard and we thought that was the greatest thing in the world. But then Kim started carrying a Bible to school and reading it during lunch. That seemed totally weird to me. And then Dave, who sat next to me in biology class, got saved. He used to pass notes to his best friend about their LSD trips. He even stole the answer card for the entire year's tests from the teacher, and I would go to his house and memorize the multiple-choice answers. Do you know how I found out he got saved? He went to the biology teacher and apologized for stealing the answers. The teacher made fun of him in front of everybody. But I thought, *Wow, Dave got saved and he's not a good person.* It rocked my world and totally turned upside down my paradigm of who was eligible for salvation!

I was so freaked out that I decided I wasn't about to get into it. The rest of our group kept its distance from the "born-againers" with their Bibles at lunch. We talked about what was happening, however, because it was making a real impact in our school. I'm embarrassed to admit it, but one day I even uttered the dumbest statement imaginable when some born-againers were walking past me. I loudly said, "Hey, I'm a Christian, okay? But I'm *never* going to be born again." I can only imagine how hard they laughed after I was saved!

My sister continued to invite me to church week-after-week. Even though I wouldn't go with her, she would come home and tell me about the services. I found myself describing her church to my friends when we would have conversations about the born-againers. I told them, "My sister goes to this really cool church. It's a Calvary Chapel and they have really good music. You can wear whatever you want (the pastor wears tennis shoes on Sunday), and there are a lot of young people." Everyone would say, "Really? You went to church?" I'd say, "Are you kidding me? I don't go to church. My sister goes to church." As I began to talk about my sister and her church, I started thinking, *This church sounds pretty good; maybe I should try it.*

It was about this same time that I was walking down the hallway at school and a girl named Debbie approached me. I had seen her around but I didn't know her at all. (As I've said, I wasn't the most welcoming person.) Debbie walked up to me and said, "Diane, I know you don't know me, but on Sunday my pastor encouraged everyone to choose somebody to pray for this week. He also said to do something nice for the person. I chose you." I was in shock that anybody "spiritual" would choose to do something nice for *me*. What the pastor probably said was, "Find the person you would never want to meet in a dark alley at night or ever tell about Jesus for fear they would get saved and you might have to spend eternity with them. And pray for that person this week."

Regardless, Debbie took his words to heart. She reached out her hand and gave me a little Precious Moments button that said something like *Love One Another.* I brushed her off in my typically cool and callous manner, so she may never know what a massive impact she made on my life with her simple act of obedience.

About a month later, I was in my Marriage and Family class at school. The teacher often threw out topics and let the class debate them. The topic he threw out that day was "Heaven or Hell." The debate got almost as hot as the topic! At one point, I stood up and said, "Listen, this hell thing is just something Christians made up to scare people. I don't believe in hell." I felt pretty bold about my statement because, after all, that's what my mom had taught me. After a few people spoke, Debbie stood up with her Bible and said, "I know everyone has their opinion here, but I thought it might be interesting to know Jesus's opinion on the subject. He actually believes there's a hell and He talked about it quite a bit." Then she opened her Bible, began reading from the Gospels, and quoted Jesus. This was extremely disconcerting information to me because if there was a hell I was pretty sure I was going there. She had gotten my attention!

That same week I was with an on-and-off again boyfriend when I ran into a guy that I had had a crush on for two years. I said, "Hey, Robert, what's up?" He answered, "Well, I'm a Christian now." Shocked, I responded, "Oh really. I'm a Christian too." Now Robert could have said, "Diane, looking at the way you're dressed, knowing you the way I do, and seeing who you're here with, I would definitely challenge you on that point." But he didn't. He was really wise. (And if you ever get the opportunity to share Christ with someone like me, remember this guy's approach because it is extremely effective.) He said, "You are?" And then added, "Isn't it great when you get up in the morning, you read the Bible, and God gives you a promise for the day. And then all throughout the day that promise helps you? And isn't it great when you're praying for somebody and they give their heart to Jesus or when God answers your prayers? And isn't it great . . . ?" and he just continued on and on. I stood there with my mouth hanging open. Unfortunately, we had to leave and the conversation ended.

When I went home I searched high and low looking for Robert's phone number because one haunting question kept replaying in my mind. I wanted to ask him, "What do you have that I don't have?" I really thought

I was a Christian. *Aren't you automatically a Christian if you were born in America and never killed anybody? I wasn't Jewish, Muslim, Buddhist, or anything like that so wasn't I a Christian by default?* After my conversation with Robert, I realized I had never read the Bible or had a promise carry me through the day; I had never prayed for anybody or seen anything happen in their life. Robert was salt to me and I was thirsty from that point on.

In the meantime, Linda was still patiently inviting me to church. She never tried to pressure me or manipulate me. One day she said, "Hey, Diane, I'm going to San Diego on Sunday. Do you want to go?" I said, "Yeah, sure." Saturday night, very late, she added, "Oh, by the way, we're going to church on the way there." She must have been shocked when I said, "Okay." And so I went to Calvary Chapel in West Covina for the first time. I made her promise to sit in the back row with me. I was so afraid that when I walked into that church I would be judged or ushered out. In the back of my mind I was thinking that if I went to church I could finally prove to her that I didn't belong there. I figured somebody would probably come up to me and say, "Uh, excuse me, but who let you in? It's time for you to leave; you're not welcome here."

Instead, I walked into a room full of smiling faces, where I sensed genuine, godly love in the air. People were singing to God as if He was really there. I didn't know people could do that. I thought we had to sing to a book. It was really exciting. Then I noticed something even more peculiar. Right in front of me was a guy who looked like he belonged to a gang sitting next to a surfer whose hair was still wet from surfing that morning. There were older people together with a lot of young people. Some guys wore ties and others wore sandals. I had never seen that kind of cross-cultural variety in church. As I thought about it, I realized I hadn't seen it anywhere in life. I remember thinking, *This is incredible!* I loved it instantly.

The pastor got up and he shared from the Word of God, but he made it fun, interesting, and exciting. I was so elated that the whole way down to

San Diego I read the little gift Bible that my sister had let me borrow for church. I read a whole Gospel, although I can't remember which one. I began going to church with my sister, and I didn't even mind if we didn't sit in the back row. It was about my third visit when it suddenly started to dawn on me that the people around me with this contagious excitement were all really "good" like my sister. I started to have a sinking feeling that maybe I was not really one of them—I had been given the opportunity before to be like them but had not followed through.

It was in third grade that I went to something called "Good News Clubs for Kids." My friend, Laura, had promised me there would be cookies and punch there. I remember the precious woman who taught us. At the second meeting she asked us if we wanted to stand before God with dirty hearts or clean hearts. She had a felt board and she placed a figure of a man with dirty, tattered clothes on it. "Do you want to stand before God wearing dirty, tattered clothes or wearing beautiful garments?" she asked. Then she put a felt figure with beautiful clothes on the board and I decided I wanted that. So with all the sincerity a nine-year-old can muster, I asked Jesus into my heart. But there was no follow-up and no one in my life to nurture that decision, so I never really grew in my relationship with Christ.

Now there I was years later sitting in church thinking, *I blew it, I had my chance. I could have been like these people and like Linda, but I didn't do it.* Without telling my sister, I decided to never step foot in a church again. Regrettably, I am known for my determination and this was no exception. I stopped going to church and got really deep into sin; my behavior was worse than ever.

I thank God that He did not give up on me! It wasn't too long after this ridiculous decision that God set the next series of circumstances into motion. My younger brother was playing Little League and my dad is such a sports fanatic that I was expected to be at every game. (If I wasn't able to attend I had to have a written note from somebody giving a good excuse for my absence.) Sitting in the stands one afternoon watching a game, I noticed a bunch of blue papers strewn all over the bleachers. I picked one up and started making paper airplanes with it. Eventually I read it and discovered that it was an invitation to a Bible study. My first thought was, *Maybe I'll try it.* Then that old hopeless, unworthy feeling came over me and I crumpled the paper up and threw it on the ground.

When I left the game, I pulled my car out of the parking lot and drove up to a red light. Another car pulled up alongside me with two guys in it. They honked their horn and began waving a piece of paper at me. I thought, *They're probably inviting me to a party. That's what I need— a party.* I rolled down the window and one of the guys started to say, "Hey, would you like to . . . ?" I was already nodding yes because I *needed* a party, but also because he was kind of cute. You can imagine my shock when he continued, ". . . Would you like to go to a Bible study?" He handed me the same blue flyer that I had just thrown away. I heard myself saying, "Yeah, I guess." For two days I wrestled with whether or not to go. Finally I decided, *Well, it can't hurt. It's not at a church. It's at someone's house. I'm going to go.*

The study was on the book of Revelation. I sat through the whole thing and didn't understand one word of what was said. But the worship and the people's expressions got to me. I looked around and thought, *These people are so lucky. They have everything I want.* At the end of the study, the leader said, "If you have any questions regarding heaven, find me tonight and let's talk."

I was like Nicodemus who went to see Jesus in the middle of the night. I waited until there was absolutely no way anyone would notice and then I found the teacher. I blurted out the question that had been lingering in my heart, "You said if we had any questions regarding heaven, we could ask you. Well, when I was nine years old I prayed the sinner's prayer, but I've lived a really bad life ever since. *Do you think I even have a chance of going to heaven?*" He responded, "Well, why don't we find out?" I was puzzled and asked, "What do you mean?" He said, "Why don't you pray and ask Jesus to forgive you for those sins and ask Him into your heart afresh?"

I had never thought of that. How crazy that the girl who was always being given second chances would think that God would be any less gracious than people had been! With a little hesitation I said, "You can do that?" He was laughing as he said, "Of course you can do that. God loves you. He brought you here specifically to let you know that. Didn't you notice that when you got here everybody moved out of the way to let you sit almost right in front of me? The Lord wanted to make sure you heard His heart." I had noticed that although the living room was packed when I arrived at the Bible study, the people had warmly welcomed me and ushered me into the middle of the room. So I did the only logical thing at that point—I said the prayer with him. It wasn't until I uttered the final amen and turned around that I realized I had not gone unnoticed at all! There were about twenty-five people watching me pray. They hugged me and welcomed me into the kingdom of God. Then they said, "Listen, one of the things you need is a really good Bible-teaching church. Do you know of any churches you might attend?" I told them I had gone to Calvary Chapel of West Covina (which is now Calvary Chapel Golden Springs), and they all started laughing as they chimed together, "That's our church!"

The amazing aspect of this story is that two weeks later the Bible study stopped meeting because the leader moved to Washington to start a church. In fact, he was supposed to leave the month before, but there was an unexplainable delay. I cry every time I think of this story because it has God's fingerprints all over it. To think that the Lord would actually hold that Bible study in place so that I could give my life to Him is so indicative of His intimate care and concern over each of our lives!

I went home and became your A-number-one typical "Jesus freak." I scared my folks, my neighbors, my classmates, and my teachers half to death. They couldn't believe the change in my life because it was so radical. I was as different as night and day. From that evening until this day I have never had a desire to smoke or drink or to do any of the stuff that I'd been involved with up until that time. God completely removed all the ungodly desires from my life. I know that doesn't happen for everyone, but that is what happened in my life. I was only in school for another month-and-a-half but God really set me apart for Himself. The change was so drastic that people began to shy away from me when they saw me coming. I had my Bible, my *JESUS SAVES* T-shirt, and stickers on my old '64 Thunderbird. I became known as a Jesus freak, and as I think back on it, I consider that label an honor.

Getting saved was just the beginning. I read Ephesians 2:10, which says: *For we are God's workmanship, created in Christ Jesus to do good works, which God prepared in advance for us to do* (NIV), and realized that before I was even saved God had a calling on my life, as He does on all of our lives. It is up to us to find our calling. I decided to volunteer at the church bookstore. I'd like to say it was because I wanted to get involved in ministry, but it was because a great-looking guy worked there and I wanted to get to know him. We actually started seeing each other, but it didn't work out and he eventually stopped working in the bookstore. Talk about God's grace—He allowed me to keep volunteering there in spite of my ulterior motive and even after my fleshly reason for doing so left! I learned that God is gentle with us as new believers. Even when our hearts are not completely right, He will bless us as He purifies our motives. I loved working in the bookstore so much that after every service I would run there to sell tapes, books, and Bibles.

I continued to grow in the Lord. I would listen to tapes whenever I could, go to church whenever the doors were open, and listen to the Christian radio to take in the Calvary Chapel pastors who were teaching the Word. I stayed in that beautiful bubble of getting to know and grow in the Lord for about a year-and-half. I was attending a junior college and for the first time in my life, I was actually trying my best in school, getting good grades, and enjoying it. However, I couldn't figure out what I wanted to do when I graduated and the indecision was really beginning to frustrate me.

One day as I sat down under a gorgeous oak tree on campus, I opened my Bible and prayed, "Lord, what is it that I am to do with my life? Don't You want to use me?" I won't say that He audibly spoke to me, but I sensed His answer in my heart: "Diane, I want to use you, but You are trying to do it for Me. What I would really like you to do is surrender. Completely lay your life down and let Me live My life through you. Then I will show you what I have for you."

That week I was baptized in the Holy Spirit. I also heard an announcement about a full-time Bible school that was starting at the church. Without a second thought, I signed up. It was almost immediately afterward that I began to experience those familiar, old sinking feelings. I started thinking that if I walked into Bible school they would usher me out into the hall and tell me that I didn't belong. And just like before, I was wrong. Pastor Raul Ries warmly greeted the students on the first day of class and said something like, "There are many reasons why God has brought each of you here. Some of you will be better moms and dads, some of you will be better employees or employers, and some of you will be pastors and pastors' wives. But whatever the reason, God will change you for the better because you have devoted yourself to the study of His Word." I can see now that from the very first day of class, God was speaking into my life the encouragement and knowledge I would need for the future He had planned for me.

After ten weeks of class we broke for a three-month summer vacation. I had the most incredible time studying God's Word and I didn't want the experience to end. The counselors at the Bible school encouraged me to participate in a practicum so I would get hands-on experience in the ministry. I really wanted to go on a missions trip to Colombia, but the Lord kept closing the door. Finally, a girl I didn't know well came to me and said, "Diane, I'm going to Las Vegas for my practicum." With a smiling face I said, "Oh, that's great." But inside I thought, *Who would want to go to Las Vegas to do ministry?* Then she asked, "Would you like to go with me?" I told her I would pray about it and walked away still stunned that anyone in their right mind would *ever want to go to Las Vegas.*

Two weeks later I was on a bus to Las Vegas. When we arrived it was one hundred and sixteen degrees outside. I couldn't wait for the evening to come and cool us down, but to my dismay, the temperature didn't change at night. I still remember the goofy outfit I wore on the bus and how awful I looked. I hadn't even bothered to put on any makeup. I only mention this because the first person that I met when I walked into Calvary Chapel of Las Vegas was Bob Coy—my future husband. He would say that when he saw me it was love at first sight. Now you know why they say love is blind! Actually it demonstrates how much of a God-thing our meeting had to be.

Bob's pastor introduced us and asked Bob to "be in charge of our lives" during our visit. (I like to add, humorously, that he's been in charge of my life ever since!) We spent that week together but didn't really get to know each other too well. I was so focused on ministry and so determined not to let anyone or anything interfere with my relationship with Jesus that I was totally clueless to the fact that he was attracted to me. We laugh about it now because, as I look back, I can clearly see all of his attempts to impress me. For example, when we met he was wearing jeans and a T-shirt, but every day from then on he wore a tie and a matching outfit. And I didn't even notice!

I did begin to notice him when I got back to California. We had decided to keep in contact and he started calling and writing to me. We built a friendship over the next few months, which was different from any I had ever experienced with a guy. One of the most important aspects of our friendship was that it did not interfere with my walk with the Lord. In fact, my relationship with the Lord grew because of my relationship with

Bob. After about eight months of a long-distance relationship, I moved to Las Vegas. Eight months later, on November 17, 1984, we were married, and eight months after that we moved to Florida to start Calvary Chapel Fort Lauderdale.

God had asked me to move out of the way so that He could dictate my future. I'm so glad I did because I would never have arrived where I am today if I had done my own thing.

I'll never forget the day after they announced our engagement at Calvary Chapel of Las Vegas. I was working in the bookstore after service and people started coming in and congratulating me. They were saying, "Oh, you're going to be a pastor's wife." I was taken aback because when I first met Bob he was not a pastor. I don't think I would have ever even considered marrying a pastor. Remember, I saw myself as the "bad girl." I knew Bob was a pastor at this point, but it hadn't dawned on me that this meant I would be a pastor's wife. The idea scared me to death. I kept wondering, *What is a pastor's wife anyway?*

Despite my fear, God kept encouraging me with Ephesians 2:10. I was His workmanship and if that meant being a pastor's wife, then He would accomplish His work through me. He reminded me that He anointed David as king of Israel when he was still a little shepherd boy. David was overlooked by everybody, and yet God made him king. However, many years passed before David realized his divine appointment as God's reigning, ruling king. In the same way, the Lord encouraged me, "Diane, I have prepared this for your life before you even came to be. I will fit you for the role. My grace is sufficient for you."

It was around the state of Texas—as we were on the way to Fort Lauderdale in the U-Haul—that it dawned on me that pastors' wives sometimes teach Bible studies. I turned to Bob in a panic and said, "Hey listen, when we get to Florida, I just want you to know that I will never, ever teach the Bible to women. I'll work in the bookstore. I'll do anything behind the scenes, but I'll never teach the Bible." He wisely said, "We'll see what God has in store."

We had been in Fort Lauderdale for about a year and the ministry was getting underway. The Lord had really been impressing on my heart that He wanted me to teach, but I kept arguing with Him. Then one night I went with my friend, Mary Anderson, to the girls juvenile detention center. We had a great night of ministry and she was dropping me off at home. Suddenly she looked at me, completely unaware of my inner struggle, and said, "I think we need a ladies Bible study. Maybe you could teach us." I burst into tears, jumped out of the car, slammed the door, and ran up to my apartment. I was terrified, but the Lord didn't let up and neither did Bob. Finally, I gave in. The strange thing is that I have been teaching Bible studies now for close to twenty years, and I can tell you that I honestly love it. It is one of the more challenging, yet rewarding privileges I have as a pastor's wife.

This has been the *Reader's Digest* version of my testimony. It would take years to read all that God has done, but I think I've shared enough to give you a glimpse of God's glory in my life. I love my story because it illustrates the truth of 1 Corinthians 2:9: *No eye has seen, no ear has heard, no mind has conceived what God has prepared for those who love him* (NIV).

Biography

Diane Coy is the wife of Senior Pastor Bob Coy of Calvary Chapel Fort Lauderdale. She is also the mother of Christian and Caitlyn Coy, who were both answers to her and Bob's ten-year-long prayer for children. Diane and Bob left Calvary Chapel of Las Vegas in 1985 with one other couple to start the ministry in Fort Lauderdale. They have had the unique experience of watching God grow their fellowship from four people in a living room to thousands on a

78-acre campus with over 400,000 square feet of facilities. Diane has overseen the women's ministry at Calvary Chapel Fort Lauderdale for the last twenty years and has taught many Bible studies and conferences. Her style and flavor are reflective of the grace and wisdom with which God has blessed her as she has walked with Him through twenty-one years of ministry.

Rosemary Gallatin

An Icy Heart Melts

"Come now, and let us reason together," saith the LORD:
"though your sins be as scarlet, they shall be white as snow;
though they be red like crimson, they shall be as wool."
Isaiah 1:18, KJV

Standing in the sanctuary praising the Lord, we sang, "This will be my story, this will by my song. You'll always be my Saviour; You will always have my heart." [1]

These words brought tears to my eyes when I reflected on the wonderful life He has given my family and me. There is absolutely no comparison between the life I have now and the life I led before January 8, 1971. That was the day I surrendered my life to the lordship of Jesus Christ. I had to do something; my previous choices were all wrong.

My first birth was May 10, 1938, in Meadville, Pennsylvania. I was the only child of Roselie and Joseph Frisina, who were both children of Italian immigrants. Mother tells me it snowed the day I was born, and maybe that was indicative of the eventual state of my heart—cold, insensitive, and hard. My father worked on the Erie Railroad as a boilermaker. When I was four years old, my dad's job took us to Marion, Ohio. Dad began to drink pretty heavily and spent much of his time in bars. Sometimes we didn't see him for days. My mother was a wonderful homemaker; however, because of Dad's drinking, she was forced to go to work as a seamstress in a plastic film company. She made things such as mattress covers and plastic pillow covers and was paid by the number of pieces she sewed. In order to support us, she worked long, tiring hours.

Mother was a perfectionist, and everything she did, she did well. Her home was impeccably clean, and her employers always rated her work high; but the one thing she could not excel at and had no control over was her marriage. Because of my father's drinking and many absences from the home, there were many legal separations, but divorce was never an option for her. The Catholic faith forbids it, and she was faithful and impeccable even in her religion. She tried very hard to transfer the fiber of her nature to me, but the pressure only caused me to rebel. I was known as a compliant child. Inwardly, however, I was defiant, and the obedience did not come from my heart.

Mother and I spent every weekend traveling by train to visit her family in Meadville. It was such fun to ride the train, and because of the frequency of our trips, the conductors knew us well. Grandma's house was so special; it was a respite from the difficulties at home, especially for my mom. Even though I couldn't understand a word of the Italian language Grandma spoke, her hugs let me know I was loved.

Because kindergarten was uncommon in those days, I started school at Greenwood Street School, a block away from our house, when I was six years old. Second grade took me to St. Mary's Catholic School on the other side of town. Our financial situation had vastly improved, and sending me to a private school topped my mother's list of priorities. School was fun, but I was more interested in friends than grades. Mine were average, and I thought "getting by" was good enough. I certainly didn't possess the desire to excel as Mom would have liked.

It was during my second year of grade school that my dad bought his first bar. This decision only increased his drinking and brought two other vices into his life: gambling and women. His profits disappeared like water down a drain, which agitated the atmosphere at home so much that I expected conflict whenever I walked through the front door. My expectation became reality. Mother began to work harder and longer, trying to survive without Dad's financial support. She would leave for work before I went to school, so I was responsible to get myself dressed, make my own breakfast, and catch the city bus at the corner of our street. Our neighbor, Mrs. Short, supervised me in the morning and when I got home from school.

Even as a child my heart was deceitful. Everyone in my class had a lunch box, but my lunch was packed in a brown paper sack with my name written on it. I was so embarrassed over this paper sack that I walked all the way home one day, ate my lunch on our front porch, and hid the paper sack in the mailbox on the corner of our street. I then went back to school thinking all was well. What I didn't know was that the mailman later found the lunch sack and, naturally, gave it to my mom.

The next day a neighbor also told her that she had seen me on the front porch eating my lunch. When my mother confronted me with the question, "Where did you eat your lunch yesterday?" I promptly lied and said I had eaten at school. I was soundly spanked, but the discipline my mother administered didn't break anything but the yardstick she had hit me with. I began to steel myself against pain, growing harder and colder as time went on.

By the time I was in eighth grade, I was occasionally stealing cigarettes from my dad. I experimented with smoking until I was fifteen years old. Then it became a habit (one that wasn't broken until I was thirty years old). We had moved to a house several blocks away from Mrs. Short, so there was no one to monitor my behavior after school. Additionally, the odor from my dad's smoking was already in the house, so I thought, *Who will know?* And since I was alone for so many hours, I would watch soap operas in the afternoons. Garbage was going into my mind, but garbage was only beginning to come out in small ways. (There would certainly be a deluge of garbage coming out of my life as I grew older.)

It was also at fifteen years of age that I met Bil Gallatin. I wasn't allowed to date yet, so we saw each other at Rexall's Drug Store where the kids gathered after school for sodas and ice cream. Bil was a junior at Harding High School, and I was a sophomore at St. Mary's. We spoke on the phone occasionally, but those phone calls were monitored closely by my mom. (I think every kid believes their parents have eyes in the back of their heads and hearing so acute that they can hear through walls!)

Finally, when I was sixteen years old, my mother allowed us to go to a Saturday matinee. Since Bil didn't have a car, we walked to the movie theatre where we saw *Pinocchio*. Bil says that for him it was love at first sight. However, it wasn't so for me. There was some sort of attraction, but I really wasn't sure what love was. I had not seen it modeled by my parents up to that point, and what I saw on the soap operas was primarily lust rather than love. Even my relationship with my parents was different from my classmates' relationships with their parents. My parents were hardly ever home at the same time. We never took vacations together and rarely ate a meal together. As a result of all these influences, my perceptions of love and family were distorted.

Bil graduated a year before me and went to college. About a year-and-a-half later, he decided to join the Marine Corps. We wrote letters frequently. His came in the mail every day, but I sent replies once a week, if that. I volunteered after school at the local hospital to see if nursing was the career I might like to pursue. After graduation in 1956 I trained at St. Francis School of Nursing in Columbus, Ohio. It was so liberating to be out of my turbulent home environment. But witnessing suffering and death right before my eyes, I again hardened myself to the pain that seemed to constantly surround me. I never cried and was told that I was unapproachable. (I later discovered this to be an accurate analysis.)

Bil asked me to marry him on Christmas Day, 1958. My parents were not thrilled with the idea. Mom suggested I find a good Italian man with lots of money. Bil was neither rich nor Italian, and the little rebel inside me became more determined than ever. We were married in September 1960. Bil worked as a technical writer for the government in Marion, Ohio. I was employed by the executive offices of General Telephone Company of Ohio as a Benefit Committee secretary. It was a visiting-nurse position, in which I investigated out-of-work employees, questioning their doctors about their prognosis and their estimated time of return to full employment. I then would report my findings to a committee that would determine whether employee benefits would be paid or denied. My job entailed a lot of traveling and overnight stays throughout the state of Ohio.

Our first son, Scott, arrived in 1961, and we could not have been happier. When Scott was only six months old, I got pregnant again. This time, I was advised to have an abortion since another child would interfere with my career. I went ahead with the abortion, which at that time was illegal. No details are necessary, except to say that I really thought I would never do that again.

Bil began to drink pretty heavily and I felt very neglected. But after all, I did have my career. Other men began to look pretty good to me, especially one man in particular. An affair ensued and continued for three years. I filed for divorce, but then one day I came to my senses and wondered what in the world I was doing. The affair and the divorce proceedings stopped, and our marriage began to mend. Bil was ignorant of the affair and still drank heavily. He was offered a job managing a clothing store in Lorain, Ohio, in the Cleveland area. We moved, and I got pregnant again, but miscarried very early in the pregnancy. I was sure God was judging me for the abortion I had had. However, I became pregnant a fourth time, and our son, Jeff, was born in March 1968.

Bil decided that we should file for bankruptcy and move to another state. We had no idea that God was working to bring us to the end of ourselves, and at the same time, was leading us to the place where we would one day give our hearts to Christ. Bil applied for a job doing construction on Disney World in Orlando, Florida, and was hired. The thought of a new life filled me with excitement. In May, when Jeff was only seven weeks old and Scott was seven years old, we sent our things ahead with movers, piled into our VW Bug, and set out on our pursuit of life, liberty, and happiness.

I kept thinking about this fresh start we would have, but it turned sour when we reached Lafollette, Tennessee. It was there that Bil announced that we were not going to Florida; we were going to California instead. I think I cried all the way to Oklahoma simply because my apple cart had been turned upside down. What I had thought was Bil's intention, wasn't his intention at all. Ever since I had known Bil, he had always been impulsive, and this was another example of his impulsiveness. Knowing this about him didn't make the decision any easier for me to accept.

We arrived in San Juan Capistrano, California, three days later, stayed in a motel for a couple of days, and instructed the movers to put our belongings in storage. We then drove up Pacific Coast Highway to Laguna Beach where we found an efficiency apartment. Bil launched out to find a job and was hired as an apprentice to a brick layer. He held that job for several months, but later was able to support us by framing houses—and he loved being a carpenter. We were quickly able to rent a home in Corona del Mar and had our things sent to the house. It was so comforting to have my things around me again.

However, Bil's addictive habits worsened. He not only continued drinking, but began taking marijuana, LSD, and other drugs, which he bought from a young man he met on the job. In addition to providing drugs, this man began to tell him about Jesus. Bil began to read the Douay Bible we had been given as a wedding present nine years earlier. The Holy Spirit revealed incredible things to him, but his drug use landed him in the Orange County Medical Center and then the psychiatric unit of Brea Community Hospital.

After Bil's discharge, he began to fellowship at Calvary Chapel in Costa Mesa. He was eager to learn God's Word and had some long talks with Pastor Chuck Smith. He was also very eager to get me to learn God's Word and began writing verses on the bathroom mirror with my lipstick. Life seemed so bizarre! Bil was having his own battles with demons, and they were working overtime on me. The more he embraced his new life in Christ, the more I rebelled. I wasn't interested in drugs, primarily because I was afraid of losing my nursing license. Instead, I had another extramarital relationship and spent weekends in Las Vegas drinking and gambling. I was plainly going the way my own father had gone and becoming the very thing I disliked in him.

> The truth of Bil's words suddenly sank deep within my spirit. Fear gripped my heart, and I thought, *What if I die on this murderous table? Will I go to heaven?*

Bil and I separated once again, and this time it looked irreconcilable. He was leaning heavily on the Lord, but the world was looking more and more appealing to me.

The affair produced another pregnancy, and on January 8, 1971, I found myself on another abortion table somewhere north of the city of Los Angeles. As I lay on the table, I thought about Bil's constant preaching that I needed to receive Jesus into my heart for the forgiveness of my sins. The truth of his words suddenly sank deep within my spirit. Fear gripped my heart, and I thought, *What if I die on this murderous table? Will I go to heaven?* As the doctor began to administer the anesthesia, I spoke quietly to the Lord, "Save me."

The ride home in the car with the baby's father was a quiet one, and I decided to end the relationship. When he agreed it brought complete relief. My heart was already turning back to the restoration of all things: my life, my marriage, and motherhood. I felt so different; it was like nothing I had ever experienced before. I was filled with a compelling desire to do the right thing. Bil was staying at the house caring for the boys during my absence, and when I got home I asked him, "Are you going to 'that' church this week?"

My desire to go with him was so strong. My choices in life had been horrible, and I knew I needed to be delivered from my misery. Driving up Pacific Coast Highway to work the next day, I found myself crying. I was grieving over the death of my baby and was remorseful over my lifestyle. Wouldn't you know a car passed by me with a bumper sticker on the back that said, *GIVE JESUS A CHANCE*—and I did!

Remember now, I was a very worldly woman. When it came time to go to church, I dressed in my finest apparel. It was a Thursday night and the small sanctuary on the corner of Sunflower and Greenville was packed. People were sitting everywhere: in the pews, on the floor, outside on a patio, and even in the entryway doors. Entering Calvary Chapel with Bil, I felt as though I was Pearl from *The Scarlet Letter*, with an "A" for adultery hanging from a string around my neck. Later I realized that I was experiencing the conviction of the Holy Spirit.

Pastor Chuck led the worship *a cappella*. He had been teaching through the book of Revelation, but on that night, just for my sake, the Holy Spirit had him go to Isaiah 1:18 and quote the most memorable verse of my entire life: *Come now, and let us reason together, saith the LORD: though your sins be as scarlet, they shall be white as snow; though they be red like crimson, they shall be as wool* (KJV). Those four scarlet letters I had imagined around my neck—two for the adultery and two for the abortions—instantly fell to the floor. After Pastor Chuck quoted this passage, I sensed a total transformation of my mind, emotions, will, and heart.

My life was converted. It was a relief to surrender to One who had more wisdom than me. The floodgates were opened and I wept in total relief from my burden of guilt. I wept out of remorse for having sinned against Bil, the boys, and ultimately the Lord, and because I had wasted twenty-nine years living for myself.

Pastor Chuck gave an altar call, and it seemed as though the work that had been started by the Lord on the abortion table was finished that night at Calvary Chapel. About twelve of us raised our hands to accept Christ and were taken aside into a little room across from the sanctuary. Pastor Chuck read through Matthew, chapter 11 with us, teaching us one by one that we had come to Jesus because we were heavy laden with sin. He said that now we were to take Jesus's yoke upon us and learn of Him; this was how we would find rest for our souls. He explained the importance of reading the Word to renew our minds and the necessity of staying in fellowship. It seems as though that day was only yesterday, but it was actually thirty-four years ago. But oh, the remembrance is so sweet and vivid in my mind!

My soul was saved just as God's Word promises in Psalm 19:7, *The law of the LORD is perfect, converting the soul.* The reality of Christ's death on Calvary *for me personally* thundered in my heart. I loved Him so much at that moment; I really thought my heart was going to burst with gratitude. From that day forward, I don't think I have ever been remiss in abounding in thanksgiving for the great price Jesus paid for me.

Bil bought me a Bible and I immediately began a quest to know the God who had done such a wonderful thing for me, and to find out what He expected of me as a wife and mother. I continued to work in the recovery room at Hoag Hospital in Newport Beach, much to the disappointment of my husband. One night as Bil was about to leave for a Saturday night men's prayer meeting, we had an argument over something insignificant—I can't even remember what it was. After he left I was listening to a teaching tape about marriage. The Holy Spirit spoke clearly to me about allowing my husband to fulfill his role in the marriage and about fulfilling God's plan for me. The speaker, Ken Gulliksen, said that mothers working outside the home can create unnecessary stresses in the marriage. God had opened my eyes to see what I hadn't seen for such a long time: He wanted me to quit work and be a homemaker. When Bil came home that night, I shared with him that God had spoken to me about quitting my job. His eyes filled with tears of joy and relief. It was a major answer to prayer for him.

However, there was still something between us that was unresolved. Later that same week I decided to be honest with him about my past. We had one of those heart-wrenching talks with lots of tears and wonderful forgiveness. We both realized that sin had caused us to grow cold in our relationship and that our love for each other was pretty much gone. In our bedroom that night, we knelt in prayer asking God to forgive us of our sins against Him and against each other. We also asked Him to restore our love. For too many years we had blamed each other for what was missing in our marriage, but now we brought ourselves to the only One who can fix the broken—Jesus—wonderful, wonderful Jesus.

We were right in the middle of the Jesus Movement revival and for about seven years we attended Calvary Chapel in Costa Mesa every time the doors were open. In 1973 Bil was asked to attend a pastors' training school, and it was then that God began to speak to him about his call into the ministry. On graduation day, men prayed over each student. When Pastor Keith Ritter and Pastor Mike MacIntosh prayed for Bil, they received a vision with an interpretation.

The vision was of a farm scene with animals grazing. A silo was standing off to one side with an open top, and there was a wagon as well. The interpretation was that Bil was the silo; the top was off because he was still being filled and was not yet ready to feed the sheep that were hungry and waiting to be fed. The wagon represented some kind of journey that would take place. I wondered about all of this and began to pray.

Bil launched out a couple of times to start a Bible study in Ohio, but we always came home to Calvary Chapel in Costa Mesa. That was our Jerusalem, our refuge.

Bil was on staff at Calvary Chapel as a carpenter for about a year, and he taught a home study every week on Lido Island in Newport Beach. In 1977 Bil felt the Lord was directing us to move to the Finger Lakes area of New York. Many things seemed to confirm the call, even an article in *National Geographic* featuring the region. When he asked me what I thought about moving to New York, I must admit the idea was not very appealing to me. I loved our church, especially the women's Bible studies, which were vital for my spiritual growth. Jeff was attending Maranatha Christian Academy and Scott went to Newport Harbor High School. Whenever I thought about pulling the kids out of school, leaving our church and all the wonderful friends I had made, it would bring tears to my eyes. I needed the Lord to change my heart.

I asked Bil not to be too hasty, but to pray and wait until the Lord did a work in me. In just thirty days, after reading the Scriptures that God had given Bil and seeing the providential circumstances that affirmed them, I knew he was called to the ministry and that we were called to move to New York. We arrived on July 7, 1977 (7/7/77), and Bil began to teach the Word in a home Bible study.

There were eight people the first night, and slowly it began to grow. The Lord was opening so many doors! Before long Bil was working as a carpenter during the day and teaching in home studies five nights a week.

We began to meet on Sundays wherever we could get space. We went from a townhouse to the basement of a bar to a banquet room at a motel to a grange hall in little, old Pumpkin Hook, New York. I would help by ministering to children, but the Lord was raising men up pretty quickly to be used where they were needed. We began prayer meetings as soon as we arrived in New York: Bil started a Saturday night men's prayer meeting in the basement of our condo, and I initiated a women's weekly prayer meeting that continues today. The Lord opened a door for a women's Bible study in someone's home, and a group of us women grew together, laughed together, and cried over our children together. God developed lasting friendships. Little by little, God added to the church such as should be saved.

One sin loomed in the recesses of my heart, however, and that was rebellion. Being a self-centered person, everything got in my way, especially God's people. Serving others was not in my nature, but it was something God wanted me to do with my life. *Surely God is punishing me*, I thought, *Why would the Lord call me to such a difficult task?* What I didn't know was that the difficulty originated with me, not with God! I soon discovered that resisting God's plan for our lives makes living difficult. His yolk is easy and His burden is light. God wanted me to be pliable in His hands, and that didn't happen overnight; it took years.

For twenty-seven years Bil quarried out precious living stones for God's purposes and I was right beside him praying on his behalf and doing what I could to help him. (I have always thought of myself as Bil's wife rather than a pastor's wife, and somehow that has made the tyranny of demands upon me a little easier to bear.)

In 2003 things began to change. I had been battling a liver disease since 1991, and that year it developed into a major crisis. In August a hemorrhage developed in my esophagus, which landed me in the intensive care unit of the hospital. Shortly thereafter, I was meeting with the liver transplant team. My son, Jeff, volunteered to be the donor, and I began having tests to prepare for the transplant. The doctors ordered a mammogram and it revealed a malignancy. The lump was removed and radiation followed. Due to the malignancy, I will not be able to have the transplant until I have been cancer-free for five years. This is very disappointing since my liver continues to deteriorate. And yet, I know that my times are in the Lord's hands and that He has a plan for me. God is my refuge and strength even though *He weakened my strength in the way* (Psalm 102:23, KJV).

Many times I find myself having to hide under the shadow of His wings until these calamities pass (Psalm 57:1). Even though I have had my family by my side at all times, the reality is that it is just me and Jesus going through this together. But I haven't just been going through all of this, I have been growing through it! He has definitely deepened the spiritual well! I don't say that in arrogance, but in gratefulness of heart, because this time there has been no resistance from me.

My circumstances have not changed to this date, as far as my health is concerned, but my acceptance of God's providence for me has. God's Word has spoken loudly to me and Don Moen's song, "God Will Make a Way," [2] ministered to me deeply during the darkest of days. My son, Scott, has said, "Mom, it's just a bend in the road." And indeed it is. God's ways certainly are not our ways, but they are always best.

Recent years have brought huge changes in Bil's ministry as well. For some time he was being invited to speak in Europe. If he remained as senior pastor of the church he had watched grow from the ground up, it would be impossible to accept those invitations. One day during my morning devotions, God clearly spoke to me. I was reading 1 Corinthians 7:29, *But this I say, brethren, the time is short: it remaineth, that both they that have wives be as though they had none* (KJV). Time is short until the return of the Lord (and until the end of our lives, as Bil and I are getting older). Because God has done so much in our lives regarding redemption and restoration, we have decided to go for the gold and finish this race well, making our lives count for His eternal purposes! Bil now spends much of his time ministering in Europe, and I am content to "stay by the stuff" at home and pray (1 Samuel 30:24).

Ephesians 2:4–6 beautifully sums up the story of our lives. May it sum up the story of your life as well!

But God, who is rich in mercy, because of His great love with which He loved us, even when we were dead in trespasses, made us alive together with Christ (by grace you have been saved), and raised us up together, and made us sit together in the heavenly places in Christ Jesus.

Biography

Rosemary Gallatin resides in Farmington, New York, with Bil, her husband of forty-five years. Bil has served as senior pastor of Calvary Chapel of the Finger Lakes for twenty-seven years and now travels extensively, speaking throughout Europe and "strengthening the brethren" there. While Bil is away from home, Rosemary enjoys time with their family, fellowshipping with the saints, quilting, and speaking at women's events. She and Bil have two sons in full-time ministry, two godly daughters-in-law, and three grandchildren who are precious blessings in their lives. With all this, Rosemary continues to look forward to new ministry opportunities and all that the Lord has in store for her.

Lenya Heitzig

Through Open Doors

Delight yourself also in the LORD,
and He shall give you the desires of your heart.
Psalm 37:4

The only things left from my college days are yearbooks, memorabilia, and flights of imagination. However, recently I had the opportunity to return to my alma mater. I jogged over the rolling hills of the Western Michigan University campus. As though on autopilot, I ran past the pond and straight to my old dorm. I walked through the musty old brick building thinking, *My time here seems like a lifetime ago.* Then it occurred to me that, not merely in quantity of years, but in quality of life, it *was* another lifetime. In those days, I was part of the "living dead." Though I had been alive physically, death reigned in my spirit. Thankfully, during my WMU days, I was born again. This new birth changed me and my life's purpose.

Though my family had an abundance of the material treasures America has to offer, I was raised without spiritual guidance since my father was an agnostic. He strongly believed in the power of *SELF* and in the power of words. When I was in high school , he wrote a book touting the power of positive thinking entitled *How to Make Your Dreams Come True*. His philosophy was summed up in the phrase, "What the mind can conceive and then believe it can achieve." In his quest for fulfillment he accumulated many things: a six thousand square-foot home complete with pool and tennis courts, a Rolls Royce, European vacations, and an extensive wardrobe. My mother never articulated her personal convictions. If she believed in a Supreme Being, she never told me. When I asked her about God, she put me in an Easter dress, neatly tied my waist-length hair into braids, and dropped me off at a neighborhood church to join Sunday school. It was a mixed signal. If church wasn't important enough for her to attend, why should I? Looking back, I think Mom believed that the here and now is all there is. Life is what you make of it. In her view, the memories of you that others possess after your death preserve the only type of immortality a person can attain. However, neither of these philosophies was sufficient to heal the wound my heart received years earlier when divorce split our family.

My parents parted ways when I was in elementary school, leaving me feeling empty and unstable. After hearing of the separation, I walked across the street to visit a widow named Maggie Rohn. She had a large porch where her English Setter, Mike, sat on guard night and day. I ran past Mike and loudly proclaimed, "My mom and dad are getting divorced." Mrs. Rohn immediately put on a pot of tea and served it using an antique china tea set she only brought out for special occasions. My childlike mind thought pretending everything was okay would make things better. But every child has to grow up. Mrs. Rohn understood the loss that I could not fully comprehend and tenderly consoled me. To this day a pot of tea brings me comfort.

My grandpa and grandma Davis's Victorian home became a haven in the midst of our family's storm. As the winds of change blew, my sister cried herself to sleep at night for many months. I abandoned my grief to comfort my siblings. I unconsciously decided to maintain control at the sacrifice of feeling anything—good or bad. For many years, that philosophy of life seemed effective.

While trying to keep up this semblance of control, I had two insatiable needs. One was to be loved by a man (or perhaps I should say, to selfishly control a man's affection). In retrospect, I can see that the loss of a father-figure left me searching to fill a gaping void. If love couldn't keep my parents together, I believed I would never be capable of loving a man enough to marry. Since I had no concept of "real love," I settled for counterfeits, going from one unhealthy relationship to another. The other coping mechanism

Something happened my sophomore year that completely upset my tenuous equilibrium. My "positive confessing" father made the most positive confession of his life: He realized he was a sinner and needed the Savior.

I relied on was seeking a good time. By the time I was old enough for college, a good time meant drinking, smoking pot, and a vulgar sense of humor. On the outside I looked like the typical Midwest co-ed of the late '70s with long, straight hair, corduroy pants, penny loafers, and a plaid shirt under a wool sweater. However, these preppie trappings couldn't contain my inner turmoil. Like many others of my generation, I self-medicated to keep up the veneer. While partying several times a week, I still pulled off a 3.5 grade point average and held down a job at a local department store. I realize now that I was a walking contradiction.

Something happened my sophomore year that completely upset my tenuous equilibrium. My "positive confessing" father made the most positive confession of his life: He realized he was a sinner and needed the Savior. He was baptized one rainy winter day at Pirate's Cove in Newport Beach, California. Philosophically speaking, I felt as though the rug had been pulled out from under me. My assumptions about life, my emotional paralysis, my disbelief in love, and my hedonistic lifestyle were now challenged by Dad's newfound faith.

Initially, I mocked my father, claiming he needed a "crutch," while I leaned on getting drunk with my friends. But when the party was over, the lights were out, and I was all alone, I was left with these questions: *What if Dad is right and I'm wrong? What if there is a God? What if heaven and hell do exist?*

I decided that if there truly was a God, I would do a little investigating. I pursued God by taking a class on Eastern religion that provided an overview of Hinduism, Buddhism, Taoism, and Islam. Of this smorgasbord of religious options, Hinduism was the most appealing because of its belief that all paths lead to God. How convenient that it accommodates hundreds of millions of gods; perhaps I could sample the "flavor of the month" god. Simultaneously, I would survey my friends' belief systems. This exposed the hollowness of those who identify in name only with one organized church or another. When I asked, "Do you believe in God?" they would respond, "I'm a Catholic," or "I go to the Lutheran church," or "My parents are Episcopalian." While attending the same party, drinking out of the same keg, and smoking the same joint as me, my pseudo-religious friends would condemn me to hell for disbelief in "their God." I watched them sit smugly secure in their church membership, without practicing the Bible's instruction. In my eyes, their empty professions portrayed Christianity as irrelevant. Throughout this period of exploration, I seemed to live in a winter of discontent—no philosophy or spiritual pursuit produced satisfaction.

Spring is the season of new beginnings. Trees and flowers that have lain dormant through the long, cold winter are resurrected. Creatures in hibernation's drowsy spell waken to a hunger for life. During spring break, the winds carried a scent of the true and living God my way. The fragrance emanated from my friend, Tamara Johnson. She was a pretty, blonde only child, full of wit and adventure. In high school, we had played in Lake Michigan's pounding surf, cheered on the freshman squad, traveled to Spain with our Spanish club, and gone on double-dates together. Then Tamara became a Jesus freak. She changed from party girl to prayer warrior. Because of her "goody-two-shoe" ways, I mocked her unmercifully and avoided her at all costs. Providentially, we both decided to attend Western Michigan University.

As I look back I marvel at a phenomenon known as "prevenient grace." The idea is that before a person can seek God, God must first have sought that person. A. W. Tozer says, "We pursue God because, and only because, He has first put an urge within us that spurs us to the pursuit. 'No man can come to me,' said our Lord, 'except the Father which hath sent me draw him,' and it is by this very prevenient drawing that God takes from us every vestige of credit for the act of coming. The impulse to pursue God originates with God." [3] Unbeknownst to me, God was pursuing me.

After one break Tamara ended up as my only companion on the three-hour drive back to WMU. I had so many questions for her. I started by saying, "My father has become a born-again Christian like you. I don't understand him anymore. What exactly do you guys believe?" Tamara's faithful practice of Christianity made me willing to listen to her. She had earned my respect because she practiced what she preached. I wish I could remember everything she said while driving past the forests, ponds, and cornfields of rural Michigan. Sitting there in the front seat of my little silver Chevy, I was intellectually intrigued by the Bible's teachings for the first time. I thought, *That makes sense.* Little did I know that listening to Tamara's explanation of God and how He had redeemed mankind through

Jesus's death on the cross was my first step toward God. Jesus said, *And you shall know the truth, and the truth shall make you free* (John 8:32). The bells of freedom had rung in my ears that day and now God was waiting for my next move—to allow the truth to set me free!

Tamara didn't try to sell the gospel cheaply, nor did she cram it down my throat. She simply told the truth, leaving me to decide how to respond. When we arrived at WMU's campus, she left me a little yellow pamphlet called *Four Spiritual Laws*. She told me to read it and call if I had any other questions.

For nearly a semester that pamphlet lay buried under homework and bills. One day my college roommates were getting high listening to the new Fleetwood Mac album, *Rumors*. I left the room because I'd had enough. I went to my bedroom to straighten up and what fell out? The *Four Spiritual Laws*. I read about the emptiness that came from man's separation from God and about how Jesus bridged the gap, reconciling us with our heavenly Father. It illustrated a life out of kilter, with "man" seated on the throne, fighting for control of his life. Then I read that if I would relinquish control, get off the throne, and let Jesus take His rightful place in my life, He would bring harmony. As I read, my frozen emotions thawed out, and I wept—something I rarely allowed myself to do. At the end, there was an invitation in the booklet for me to pray to receive Jesus as Lord of my life. I knew in the depths of my being that it was the right thing to do. I said the prayer out loud with tears streaming down my cheeks. There were no stained glass windows, organs playing hymns, or bolts of lightening. Just Lenya, at long last, surrendering control of her life to God.

At that moment my roommate, Pam, barged into the room looking for a backgammon partner. She stopped dead in her tracks when she saw me crying and asked, "What's wrong?" I said, "Nothing's wrong. I read this flyer and said the prayer at the end, and it made me cry." She read the tract just as I had, but didn't have the same response. She said, "What makes you think you'll go to heaven and I won't?" Amazingly, the same thing that comforted me threatened her. Just weeks prior I was condemned to hell for disbelief in the existence of God and now her pseudo-religious trappings seemed shabby. All I had done was say a prayer. I told her, "I don't know. It just made sense." She dragged me out to the others who thoroughly interrogated me. I couldn't answer their questions or quell their apprehensions—I'd never read the Bible. I had merely responded to the truth in that little yellow pamphlet.

That was only the first step of many on my journey to knowing God. For me, becoming a Christian was a process, not a single prayer. In the Bible, James tells us, *Draw near to God and He will draw near to you* (James 4:8). As I responded to God's initiations, I got closer to Him. That day in my room, I said yes to God. But salvation consists of more than just saying yes to God. We must also say no to our sins. Honestly, I didn't know what things to avoid and what things to pursue. I wanted my faith to be genuine. I also sensed that God wanted to transform me into His likeness by changing me thoroughly—no more shallow veneers. God wanted to clean out the rubble of my past and invade my empty heart with His love. My next step toward Him came on my summer break.

When final exams ended, I headed for California to spend the summer with my dad and his wife, Nedra. Things were changing in their hearts and home. With a hunger for God's Word they had begun attending Calvary Chapel in Costa Mesa, California. On a sunny California day, I joined them for my first service at Calvary. I remember that when we passed the bean fields near Fairview Road, I spotted a billboard that boldly proclaimed: *Maranatha, Jesus is coming soon!* The Spirit within me leapt with the same excitement one experiences riding a roller coaster.

The parking lot bustled with activity. The unpretentious, sprawling building was teeming with life in every sense of the word. More people frequented this edifice on Sunday than lived in my hometown of Ludington, Michigan, whose population neared 9,000. The place was magnetic! When I walked through the doors I knew I had found my spiritual home. The inviting, casual demeanor of the church members disarmed me. The people were laid-back and young, yet filled with vitality. Some were longhaired, barefooted hippies toting big, black Bibles, their faces adorned with expressions of unspeakable joy. These people weren't just paying their religious duty. They were hungry for Bible study, as well as one another's company, and lingered long after the service ended. I found myself desiring both their hugs and their company.

When Pastor Chuck Smith entered the sanctuary, his electric smile and glowing personality beamed with the love of God. His strong yet meek demeanor made him approachable and authoritative. He seemed genuine, not at all like one of those TV preachers I had seen. As Chuck shared from the pulpit that morning, I was overcome by his knowledge of the Bible and its Author. He didn't merely know *about* God, he knew *Him*! Chuck's style of methodically covering the Bible verse-by-verse was balanced and thorough, meeting my need to have things explained intellectually. He was—and continues to be—simple yet profound, ancient in context but relevant for today, intellectually provocative yet spiritually stimulating. The genuine warmth of Chuck's delivery made me feel like I was listening to a story on my father's lap.

After years of starvation of the soul, I had a voracious appetite. This was the first spiritual meal of my life and it was delicious! I felt fully satisfied, yet hungered for more. St. Bernard of Clairvaux wrote:

> "We taste Thee, O Thou living Bread,
> and long to feast upon Thee still;
> we drink of Thee, the Fountainhead,
> and thirst our souls from Thee to fill." [4]

Throughout the summer, I regularly attended Calvary and dined on a balanced diet of God's Word. Every Sunday morning Pastor Chuck would invite new believers to come forward to pray with the pastoral staff, but I was too ashamed to join the many others who had made their way to the altar. But I could not escape a pervading sense of being dirty, unacceptable, and separated from God. Determined to find the cleansing and closeness I desired with God, I eventually left my seat on a painful journey to the prayer room. As I walked down the aisle, each step increased my burden to an unbearable degree. I thought that everyone present could see how unworthy I was.

Pastor Malcolm Wild greeted me in the prayer room. I told him of my experiences and he asked a probing question, "Have you repented of your sins?" I was unfamiliar with biblical terms and thought repentance meant to wear a large sign warning, "The end of the world is near!" I told Malcolm, "I have no idea what that is." He said, "Repentance means to have a change of heart and direction; to turn from sin and toward God." Then he quoted Isaiah, *"Come now, and let us reason together," says the LORD, "Though your sins are like scarlet, they shall be as white as snow"* (Isaiah 1:18). I had been too ashamed of my past to accept God's mercy, but this passage let me know that God was ready and willing to cleanse anything!

As Malcolm spoke, tears began to run down my face. My cold and in-control veneer was finally melting. He asked, "Would you like to pray now for forgiveness?" I could only nod my head in agreement. With wavering voice and shaking hands, I followed Malcolm in a prayer that set me free from sin and its destructive companion—shame. A sense of absolute relief and joy swept over me. My feelings of unworthiness never returned. My heart became like a fresh page. I had a chance to rewrite the story of my life.

My fresh start began with an inkling dancing somewhere in my mind and a desire freshly planted in my heart. You see, never before had I experienced such delight and contentment in a pursuit as I had in seeking God. King David said, *Delight yourself also in the LORD, and He shall give you the desires of your heart* (Psalm 37:4). I now understand that as I worshiped Jesus, learned His ways, and obeyed His commands, He began to cultivate desires in my heart that were *His very own!* My greatest desire was to become a pastor's wife. The amazing thing was that this newfound desire seemed natural, as though my whole life I'd been inscribing dreams of marrying a pastor in my notebooks and picturing my future following that path. I assumed that every Christian woman wanted to be a pastor's wife until one day I told my roommate of my longing. She looked at me like I was crazy and shouted, "No way!" She simply couldn't relate. Apparently, this was a desire God had planted in *my* heart and mind.

I'd never met Kay Smith or any other pastor's wife. I didn't have the slightest idea of what one did. Nonetheless the hunger increased. There was only one problem: I didn't know any available pastors. But God did.

There was an immediate and mutual attraction the day I met Skip Heitzig at a backyard barbecue in Costa Mesa. I was a new Christian and this was the first party I'd been to in years without a keg of beer as the main attraction. Skip recalls that, apart from my tan skin and sun-kissed hair, watching my relaxed, direct interaction with others at the party intrigued him. His long hair was still wet from surfing in the Pacific. He had on shorts, flip-flop sandals, and rose-colored glasses. I was attracted to his incredible wit, not to mention his tall, handsome physique. Finally, I walked over to him, shook his hand, and said, "Hi, I'm Lenya." Then I sat beside him, propping my bare feet up on his chair. As we talked, our intense dialogue stimulated him both spiritually and intellectually since I was bursting with many theological questions. He recounts that, having been raised with three rowdy brothers, he was uncomfortable making friends with women, but I somehow put him at ease. I was so relieved to meet a Christian man who was young, fresh, and lively.

Skip asked me to join him at a Randy Stonehill concert that coming Saturday night at Calvary Chapel. Afterward, we ate at the Cannery Restaurant in Newport Beach and walked on the beach talking about creation and whether rock-and-roll music was redeemable. We continued to date during the season of my childhood of Christianity. Skip was always candid, disarming in his zeal for and knowledge of God. I was young and hungry for the things of God, attending services and Bible studies six nights a week. But in my immaturity, I was rough around the edges. During those early days of dating, I was embarrassed to pray publicly and my sense of humor needed adjustment. Skip was the instrument of God's loving admonition, encouraging me to speak to God as one speaks to a close friend. He also rebuked me when it came to my inappropriate language. God was in the process of renovating my life and used Skip as a tool to help refine me.

From the first time they met, my dad was confident that Skip was the man I would marry. "There's something special about that guy; God's going to use him," Dad said. It was hard to believe because a year after Skip and I had met, our relationship changed course, and we went our separate ways. Skip didn't want anything, even a relationship, to distract him from serving God with all his heart. I knew that I wanted to know God intimately and grow into a mature, godly woman, so I joined Youth With A Mission (YWAM) in Hawaii. I attended an intensive and interactive discipleship school and learned the breadth of serving Christ by serving others, the depth of intercessory prayer, and the height of self-abandoned worship. Filled with the Spirit, I discovered God had given me the gifts of teaching and administration. I participated in dramas for street evangelism, prison visitation, and acted as the single women's counselor. I was not just learning about God, I was getting to know Him experientially.

About a year later Skip and I met again when I returned to California for Christmas vacation. We bumped into each other at a friend's house and decided to have dinner. I couldn't contain my zeal for God and poured out my heart for ministry to Skip. He was taken aback and intrigued all at once. At one point he stopped me and said, "You're ministering to me! I'm amazed at how you've changed. You're such an encouragement." When he took me home I prayed out loud with passion and confidence, unlike our earlier experiences together.

After this encounter, we both began to regret that our relationship had not continued. When the holidays were over, I headed back to Hawaii to fulfill my commitment as secretary for the Discipleship Training School. At YWAM I was invited to join several mission teams to places like Thailand and Indonesia, but the Lord would not let me go. I still had a burning desire to be a pastor's wife. The idea of going to a community with no strong Bible teaching and pouring my heart into that work was overwhelming. I wanted to invest God's Word into the life of His sheep and watch the people of God do the work of God. I longed to see God's Spirit ignite a community with His love and power like He had done in Southern California during the '70s. I told my missionary friends that my gifts were more suitable for discipleship than evangelism and declined their invitations to go overseas.

The problem I still faced in fulfilling these desires for church planting was that I wasn't married to a pastor! That's when God intervened, using some key people in my life. The first people He used were my mentors at YWAM, Dave and Debbie Gustaveson. I had observed their marriage and ministry and knew I wanted a partnership in the ministry similar to theirs. Their example of selfless service to God and others made it easy to heed their counsel.

Dave and Deb knew I needed to get on with my life and make a commitment for the future. I simply could not stay in a mission organization and not serve on the mission field. Dave told me, "If this desire to be a pastor's wife is from the Lord then He will provide a pastor for you to marry. If not, it's an unhealthy fantasy that must be abolished." I told them about Skip Heitzig, who was the man I held as a standard for others in regard to godliness. I spoke of his unquenchable love for God's Word, his library full of commentaries, and his talent to lead worship. I told them how he had taught several Bible studies in the past and had already filled in as pastor of Calvary Chapel of South Bay when they were in transition between pastors. Then I said, "There's one obstacle. Skip's not interested in me."

They challenged me to send Skip an upfront letter exposing my heart and then to leave the results in the hands of God. With great fear and anticipation I wrote Skip the most vulnerable letter of my life. I told him of my vision for church planting in untilled soil. I revealed my heart for the poor and outcast and my hope to ignite a church that had a heart for the mission field. I spoke of my desire to equip the people of God with His Word and Spirit. I dropped the letter in the mail with this promise from Proverbs tucked in my heart, *Trust in the LORD with all your heart, and lean not on your own understanding; in all your ways acknowledge Him, and He shall direct your paths* (Proverbs 3:5–6).

Not surprisingly, God was simultaneously working in Skip's heart. After our reunion dinner, Skip had begun to look at me with new eyes. I had matured in the Lord, and he felt that perhaps he was shortsighted in ending our relationship. But he wondered if it was too late—maybe he had burned the bridge to my heart. When Skip received my letter, it only confirmed his regret for letting me go. He has described it as uncanny—like reading something he had written to himself. Our hearts' passion and call were becoming one.

Soon after that, Skip was returning home from his job as a radiological technologist at Westminster Hospital to his bungalow in Huntington Beach. Taking off his white lab coat, he heard his phone ring. It was the second mediation that helped bring us together. My father was on the line, and unbeknownst to me, Dad had decided to take matters into his own hands in order to guard my heart. He said, "Skip, this is Dr. Farley—Lenya's dad. She's got some difficult decisions to make. I think she doesn't feel released from you. If she could have her dream come true, you would be her knight in shining armor. If you're interested in her, I think you should let her know. If you're not, then tell her so she can move on." Skip was shocked. After praying, he decided he would attempt to regain my heart.

My answer to that vulnerable letter came about a week later. I was at work when my roommates called me to come upstairs. "I'm busy right now; it will have to wait," I responded. "There's a surprise for you," they beckoned, coming and grabbing me by the hands, dragging me to my

room. Sitting on the windowsill was a grand bouquet of exotic roses signed
with the simple note, "Skip."

Six months later, after a whirlwind courtship and wedding, I found myself in Skip's blue Datsun pick-up truck, headed for our new life together
in New Mexico. Our journey was interrupted every five hundred miles to
add oil to our smoking vehicle, which was pulling everything we owned
behind us in a U-Haul trailer. As we drove, we prayed and chatted about
our hearts for God, His Word, and His church. We couldn't wait to begin
a Bible study in Albuquerque. We had no idea that we were embarking
on the spiritual ride of our lives!

New Mexico was ready and ripe for the harvest. Our little Bible
study went from six people the first night to about two hundred people
in the first year. Many people criticized us for not doing things the
"traditional" way, but God blessed us anyway. I believe God was waiting for the right people to be in the right place at the right time, who
would get out of the way so He could do God-sized things. He had a
plan that was "exceedingly, abundantly above all I could ask or hope"
(see Ephesians 3:20).

I never could keep up with what God was doing in New Mexico. He was
always a step ahead of us. I remember the first Sunday we moved into our
third building as a result of rapid church growth. Amazingly, the new facility
was packed despite the fact that we thought we had allowed room to grow.
Walking into the service I thought, *Where do all these people keep coming
from?* Ultimately over two decades, Calvary of Albuquerque expanded
into a 20-acre campus and birthed new churches in cities throughout the
Southwest, the United States, into Canada, and overseas.

One beautiful snapshot from my journey in Albuquerque was the birth
of Women at Calvary, a Bible study that met every Tuesday morning
and evening. Requests for our homework led us to publish the Pathway
Bible study series through Tyndale House Publishing. Our first book,
Pathway to God's Treasure: Ephesians, won a Gold Medallion Award

from the Christian Booksellers Association. Our Bible studies, *Pathway to God's Plan: Ruth & Esther* and *Pathway to Living Faith: James*, soon followed.

But the Heitzigs' journey is far from over. God continues to call us to serve Him in surprising ways. In 2004 we made the difficult decision to leave the work we had started in Albuquerque twenty-three years earlier to relocate back to Southern California — returning through the door we had left. God faithfully pointed the way to Ocean Hills Church in San Juan Capistrano through several acts of providence. For me there was no place like Albuquerque, but God unexpectedly and dramatically shifted my heart.

Although our place of ministry has changed, and though the congregation is a different one, our immutable God remains faithful. The One who said, *Behold, I make all things new* (Revelation 21:5), has granted a new opportunity for adventure so we can "behold His wonders" (see Isaiah 29:14). Our new life in San Juan Capistrano holds its own challenges and blessings. I continue to use my gifts of teaching and administration for the kingdom of God. And happily, I still serve alongside my husband in ministry, continually learning new lessons and growing in the grace and knowledge of the Lord.

Biography

Lenya Heitzig is the wife of Skip Heitzig, senior pastor of Ocean Hills Church in San Juan Capistrano, California, and founding pastor of Calvary Chapel of Albuquerque, New Mexico — which, over two decades, grew to become the largest church in New Mexico, and which birthed churches in the United States, Canada, and overseas.

Lenya is a dynamic and gifted Bible expositor who fills her messages with spiritual insight, humor, and tenderness. In 1984 she launched Women at Calvary at Calvary Chapel of Albuquerque, which ministers to over 1,000 women each week. She is the director of Pathways for Women at Ocean Hills Church, and of Southwest Women's Festival, an outgrowth of the Franklin Graham Festival. Lenya continues to use her writing gift to create spiritual resources for women. She and Skip have one son, Nathan, who serves as associate high school pastor at Ocean Hills Church.

June Hesterly

Married at Sixteen

*"But you shall receive power when the Holy Spirit has come
upon you; and you shall be witnesses to Me in Jerusalem,
and in all Judea and Samaria, and to the end of the earth."*
Acts 1:8

When I gave my heart and life to Jesus Christ as a little girl, I could never have imagined that before my thirtieth birthday I would believe I had no reason to live. I began with honorable hopes and dreams, and yet, throughout my young life, I lacked the power to fulfill them.

I was born in El Centro, California, in 1941, the year World War II broke out. I think it may have been an overnight stop for my parents on their way to Santa Ana, California, where I was raised amidst the orange groves and bean fields that were common to the area in those days. My dad was the first civilian employee of the El Toro Marine Corps Air Station in Orange County.

My mother was born in Boaz, Alabama, the fifth of six girls. When she was fourteen years old, her mother died, and from then on she was raised by her alcoholic father. As far as I know she had no spiritual heritage. On my father's side, however, I have a very rich spiritual heritage. His ancestors were French Huguenots. They stole away in a pickle barrel to come to the United States so that they could freely practice their religious faith. My dad was born and raised in Albuquerque, New Mexico, and was the youngest of six children. He rebelled against the legalism and strict denominational rule of my grandmother's Nazarene church, and he did not receive Jesus as his Savior until much later. Even though neither of my parents knew the Lord, ours was a happy home filled with laughter.

Although I did not know her well, I was a little fascinated by my dad's mother. Grandmother never wore jewelry or makeup, not even face powder. Her hair came down to her knees, and she would wind it up with little tortoise shell pins. She was an ordained minister in the Nazarene denomination. She had a wonderful evangelistic ministry and would travel throughout Arizona and New Mexico planting small churches. After Sunday morning services, she would drive to various prisons, where she would preach the gospel to captive audiences. She even developed an evangelistic pen pal friendship with the famous gangster, John Dillinger.

Grandmother believed in an inaccurate version of the doctrine of sanctification, which teaches that after salvation the Christian can attain a state of sinless perfection. She actually believed she did not sin anymore, and while this certainly wasn't true, she really was a godly woman and I greatly admired her.

For one week each year, our home was turned upside down by Grandmother's presence. Both of my parents smoked, and when Grandmother came for her yearly visit, my mother would go into the bathroom, light up a cigarette, and blow the smoke out the bathroom window, supposing that Grandmother wouldn't know. My mother would also sneak me out of the house to go to my tap dancing lessons, and when Grandmother was there, we were not allowed to listen to the radio or watch television because she believed these things were of the Devil.

When I was seven years old, her visit turned our lives upside down for good. Before we were allowed to go to bed at night, my dad, my mom, my younger brother, my younger sister, and I would all be lined up in front of the sofa on our knees, and Grandmother would preach the gospel of salvation "unto God" for an entire hour. I could not understand in my little mind why God needed to be saved. Of course Grandmother was not preaching to God at all; she was preaching to all of us because we needed to hear the gospel and we needed to know Jesus as our Savior!

One night after Grandmother's preaching, my mother—much like the apostle Paul on the road to Damascus—was wakened in the middle of the night by a vision of Jesus standing at the side of her bed. She immediately slipped to the floor onto her knees and gave her heart and life to Jesus.

Afterward, our home and family were radically changed. My mother began to take us children to an evangelical church a few miles from our home. It was a Bible-preaching church—not a teaching church, but a preaching church. And so I heard the gospel. One Sunday when I was seven years old, sitting at the back of the church, and with what must have been the tenth chorus of "Just As I Am, Without One Plea" filling the air, I got up out of my seat, made my way to the front of the church, and gave my heart and life to Jesus. I was promptly baptized in water: submerged in the name of the Father, the Son, and the Holy Ghost. All I knew about the Holy Spirit was that He was called the "Holy Ghost," and at that young age that seemed a little spooky to me.

I began what today would be called a "works trip." Our pastor taught that salvation is through grace and faith in Jesus Christ, but we were taught to work very hard in our little church. Because there were probably only fifty people in the congregation, everyone had a job and was expected to serve. I absorbed the idea that I needed to be working hard in order to be acceptable to the Lord, and I was a child who wanted to be acceptable—I wanted to be a good little Christian girl. I always felt like I was standing outside a house looking into the windows at everybody else having a good time, and I believed that if I didn't work hard enough and pray enough, or give enough, then maybe the Lord wouldn't let me inside His house, His kingdom.

The works trip I was on led to an up and down relationship with the Lord. Every Sunday our pastor would preach one of two messages—because he only had two: "You must be born again," and, "Go into the world and make disciples." He knew everyone in the church (he'd known them for years), and he knew who was born again and who wasn't. At the end of every sermon, he would tack on this little blurb: "If you've done something wrong this week, you need to come forward now and rededicate your life." When I was feeling terribly sinful and would doubt that I was a Christian, during that tenth chorus of "Just As I Am, Without One Plea," I would get up and make my way down the aisle to rededicate myself to the Lord. I didn't realize I was just rededicating my flesh when in fact my flesh needed to die. (To be honest, sometimes I would look at my pastor standing at the altar all alone, and being tenderhearted, I would go forward because I felt sorry for him.) I was very young and yet I was on a spiritual rollercoaster based not upon the truth of Scripture, but upon my own feelings of failure and inadequacy.

> I always felt like I was standing outside a house looking into the windows at everybody else having a good time, and . . . if I didn't work hard enough and pray enough, or give enough, then maybe the Lord wouldn't let me inside His house.

When I was sixteen years old there was a youth rally in our community at which all the churches from Orange County were gathered together. I met a young Marine there named Jim Hesterly. He had been granted forty-eight hours leave from the military base at Twentynine Palms, California, and had called his sister and said, "Would you take me someplace where I can meet some chicks?" Slyly, she responded, "I've got just the place for you!" She brought Jim to the youth rally, and that night before the evening was over, I was sharing a hymn book at the piano with this young man who looked just like James Dean. Later my mother picked me up to drive me home. Being the good mother that she was, when she realized that a young man (Jim) was following us, she promptly lost him! His sister, however, gave him my address.

About two months later I got a letter from Jim. It was postmarked from Okinawa, Japan, where he would be stationed for a year. He asked if we could write to each other, and we began a pen pal relationship. After his tour of duty, he was discharged and returned to his home in Orange County. Jim drove a brand new, shiny, black Ford Fairlane, and boy, was I impressed! We began dating and he often picked me up after school. When my girlfriends saw this handsome boy picking me up in his shiny new car, they were impressed too.

We dated for six months, and then we were married. I was sixteen years old and he was twenty-one years old. When I was seventeen years old I gave birth to my first child and named him James, after his father, and when I was nineteen years old I had my second child, a girl named Robin. I was a child having children and I knew nothing about marriage or motherhood. The information that is available today was not available then. We did not have good Christian books. We had the Bible, but in my church, we were only taught two things from the Bible. We weren't taught from God's Word how to raise our children.

I was probably considered a "screamer" in our neighborhood. If I was raising my children today the way I raised them then, I would probably be arrested for child abuse. Because I did not know how to discipline them properly, I would get out of control and then would run to my bedroom, slam the door, and throw myself across the bed, weeping. I'm sure the neighbors thought I was a terrible mother. I certainly thought I was the worst mother who had ever lived. But remember, I had wanted to be a good, little Christian girl, and now I wanted to be a good Christian woman. I felt so inadequate in my roles as a wife and mother and in my walk with the Lord. I was still on a spiritual rollercoaster.

My husband was raised with the same denominational background as me, so we both continued the pattern of working hard in the church we were attending. We were there every time the doors were open. Our children, many a night, would fall asleep on the front pew of the church. Whenever we were asked to be on a committee, we would say yes because we didn't know how to say no. My husband served as an elder, a deacon, and the bus pastor. Every Saturday morning, he would take out his "blue bumblebees" (toys that spun on a string and made a loud screeching sound) and his bubblegum, and he would go door to door inviting the kids in the neighborhood to ride the "Blue Bible Bus" to Sunday school. The following morning, he would collect all the children and bring them to church. Then he would teach them, load them back on the bus, and take them home. And so we were very, very busy, but very, very empty. Working hard, serving hard, doing what we thought would be pleasing to God, but experiencing a profound emptiness.

When I was twenty-eight years old, the most traumatic event of my entire life occurred: The one who I loved more than anyone else in the world—more than my husband or my children—was diagnosed with malignant melanoma. My mother had discovered a mole on her back that was cancerous. She was only forty-six years old. In those days there was not much doctors could do about melanoma. By the time it was diagnosed, it had gone to her brain and she quickly deteriorated.

I had heard on the "spiritual grapevine" that God could heal. However, we didn't believe in supernatural healing in our church. We didn't pray for the sick. We didn't believe in the gifts of the Spirit. We didn't much believe in the Holy Spirit at all. I knew He was called the Comforter, but I thought that He only comforted important people like Billy Graham. I didn't think He would bother with me. However, I knew that He could heal so I began a bargaining process with Him.

I would plead, "Lord, would You please heal my mother? Please God! If You will heal my mother, I will serve You more; I will work even harder." You see, my mother was my best friend. Growing up, I was not like most teenagers who did not want to be seen in public with an adult. I loved being with my mother. We would shop together and trade clothes. She was always there for me. When I had a date, she was the one who would lie awake at night waiting for me to come home. I would come into her bedroom and sit on the end of her bed, telling her all the details of my date. Every night, no matter how late it was, she would sit in her chair and I would sit at her feet, and she would patiently pin-curl my hair. (This was before hot-rollers and curling irons were invented.) Every week she'd roll out her Singer treadle sewing machine and make me something new to wear. She was a wonderful seamstress and had exquisite taste in clothing.

I loved being with my mother and now she was diagnosed with this terrible cancer. I watched her go through such agony and suffering. I would call out daily to the Lord to heal my mother. And then, one day, after about three months, I realized that she was not going to get well. I called out to the Lord and said, "Lord, if You're not going to heal my mother, would You please take her home. I can't stand to see her suffer anymore." At two o'clock that morning, a call came from St. Joseph's Hospital in Orange, California. She had been taken to the emergency room, and I was told, "If you want to see your mother one more time, you need to come immediately."

I jumped in my car and hurried to the hospital. When I got off the elevator, I was met by a nurse. She said that my mother had "expired." I did not know what she meant by the word *expired*. I thought only magazine subscriptions or prescriptions expired. People didn't expire. Finally I understood that she was telling me my mother had slipped into the arms of Jesus.

When my mother was born again, she was radically born again and filled with the Holy Spirit. She was in love with Jesus. Her death was a bittersweet event for me. It was sweet because I knew my mother had gone to meet Jesus; she would see the One she loved face to face. It was a bitter event because I had never lost anyone whom I had loved before. I began to experience a devastating grief that was like nothing I had ever known. I would sit on the back porch of my house and cry out to God, "Lord, why did You take my mother? This is not fair, God. Why did You take her and leave me here?"

Many times when we are in a vulnerable position the Enemy will attack. He began to fill my mind with thoughts of suicide. I had a wonderful husband who loved me and two wonderful children. We had just bought our first home. Jim was a district sales-manager for Pepsi Cola Company, and he was rising in his career. We were doing well financially. But I didn't think I had any reason to live and I began to think of ways to take my own life. In my warped and twisted thinking, I started to contemplate, *If I do it "this" way, then maybe I can slip it past God and He will think it was an accident.* That's a little ridiculous. I also began to think of ways I could do it that wouldn't embarrass my family. I didn't want them to be hurt. And then, I think because the Lord has a sense of humor, something absurd stopped me. I am probably known in my family as an obsessive-compulsive housekeeper. I vacuum my carpet every single day, no matter how hectic my schedule might be. And I have to be honest: there are times that I do not even plug it in. I just move it across the floor because I like to have lines in the carpet! What prevented me from going ahead with any of my plans was the realization that if I attempted suicide and lived, I would have to clean up the mess!

It wasn't too long after my mother had died that our pastor announced a training course in preparation for a Billy Graham Crusade that would be held at Anaheim Stadium. Volunteers would be taught how to do door-to-door evangelism. I said to myself, *Hallelujah. All my life I have been instructed to go into all the world and make disciples, but no one has ever given me tools or told me how to do it.* I wanted to be a witness to the lost, but there was no love, no joy, no peace, no gentleness, no kindness, no fruit of the Spirit whatsoever in my life, and I would get tongue-tied whenever I tried to share the gospel. I would think, *What do I have in my life to share? There's no victory. How can I be a witness to the lost?* Up until that point, I had never talked to anyone about Jesus and I had been a Christian for twenty years.

I said, "I'm going to that meeting!" I got a babysitter and dragged Jim kicking and screaming all the way there. Before the instructor could take us through the little *Four Spiritual Laws* booklet that would teach us how to be a witness, he showed us a little blue booklet that had a white dove on the front. It was entitled *Have You Been Filled with the Spirit?* If he had talked about being baptized with the Spirit, I would have equated that phrase with something highly Pentecostal—like people swinging on chandeliers and rolling around on the floor. And I would have gotten out of there as fast as possible. But he talked about being filled with the Spirit and I could receive that.

He showed us page-by-page and step-by-step what it means to be filled with the Spirit. He drew three little circles, and inside each circle was a stick-figure chair that looked like a lower-case "h." In the first circle, sitting on top of the little chair, was a little cross surrounded by words like love, joy, peace, gentleness, kindness, meekness, and longsuffering—words that are used in Galatians 5:22–23 to describe the fruit of the Holy Spirit. The instructor said, "This is the person who has Christ in their life, and

Christ is sitting on the throne of their life. This is the Spirit-filled Christian." Inside the next circle was the same little chair, but the cross was outside the circle, and inside it were words like adultery, fornication, anger, envy, jealousy, malice, and wrath—all the attributes of the flesh listed in Galatians 5:19–21. This circle represented what Scripture calls "the natural man," the one who is not born again. Christ is not in their life at all. The third circle had the same little chair, but the cross was floating in the circle near the edge, and inside the circle were those same works of the flesh listed in the second circle. There was an "s" on the little chair to represent "self." Self was on the throne. This circle represented the carnal Christian, the one who has invited Jesus Christ into their life, but their flesh is in control.

I felt as though a light went on in my spirit and my mind for the very first time in my life! No one had ever told me that I could be or needed to be filled to overflowing with God's Spirit. I thought that was only for big time dudes. And I wanted desperately, now, to be in the first circle with Christ sitting on the throne of my life.

We were told that before we prayed the prayer at the end of the little booklet, we should go home and make a "sin list." Now I'm not saying this is necessary for everyone, but it was very important for me. We were instructed to ask the Holy Spirit to bring to our remembrance anything that needed to be confessed, and we were told to be very specific. Up until this point, every night, and several times during the day, I would hysterically confess my sins to the Lord and ask Him to forgive them corporately, but no one had ever told me that I needed to pray, "Lord, forgive me for this specific sin or that specific sin." I learned that I needed to keep a short account with God. I was carrying around twenty years of baggage, so it is no wonder that I was weighted down with guilt and shame.

That night I went home and took a pencil and paper to my bedroom. My husband met me in the hall and said, "You go into that bedroom and take as much time as you need." You see, he had still not gotten it. In his mind what we had learned was about me and my problems. I went into the bedroom that night and did business with God for the very first time in my life. I was desperate for the reality of God in my life. Either He was exactly who He said He was or He was nothing to me.

I asked the Holy Spirit to reveal to me the things that I needed to clean up in my life. He was very, very sweet and gentle with me. He reminded me of those times that my husband had come home and asked me, "Who ate all the cookies?" And with the chocolate still in my teeth, I would look him straight in the eyes and say, "Oh, the kids ate them." I wrote that one down.

Then He reminded me of the times that I had gone to the market and come out with too much change, and instead of returning it, I had kept it and proclaimed, "Praise the Lord!" I wrote that one down. Then He took me to another level and reminded me of all the times I had been so angry with my children, screaming and yelling at them. I wrote that down. He reminded of the times that I had been angry because I had been saving some of the grocery money to buy myself something pretty to wear, and lo and behold, the children would come home with torn knees in their jeans, and I would have to use the money I had saved to buy them new ones. (Remember, I was very young and selfish, as many of us are in those years.)

Then He reminded me of all the times I had been angry with my husband. Outwardly it would seem that I had completely forgiven him, but inwardly I would remember every detail of our problem. As wives, we have ways of punishing our husbands, don't we? We can say everything is forgiven and yet we can subtly "make them pay for their crimes." I wrote that one down.

And then He took me to an even deeper level. He said, "June, I want you to know that you've been angry with your mother." I thought, *Angry with my mother? How do you get angry with a dead person?* Again He said, "You've been angry with your mother." I agreed, "Yes, Lord, I have been angry with my mother." She had deserted me. Logically I knew that was not true, but I felt abandoned. My mother, who had always been there for me, had left me to suffer intense grief all by myself, and I was angry with her.

And then the Holy Spirit took me to the deepest level of all, to the heart of everything. He said, "June, you've been angry with Me." I literally gasped because I did not know anyone in the Bible who had ever been angry with God and had lived. However, true repentance means agreeing with God. I said, "Lord, You're right. I've been angry with You all these years. Things did not turn out the way I had anticipated in my life. I didn't plan on getting pregnant before marriage and then getting married at the age of sixteen. Lord, I thought I was going to be a missionary, and here I am with these children, with this man, in an ordinary life, and a mother who is gone. Lord, why? Why did this happen?" Again I said, "You're right, Lord, I've been angry with You." I wrote all of these things down.

We were told at the training course that once we had made the list, we were to claim the promise of 1 John 1:9: *If we confess our sins, He is faithful and just to forgive us our sins and to cleanse us from all unrighteousness.* Don't you love that word: *all*? I went down my list one by one and prayed, "Lord, forgive me for being out of control with the children and for being dishonest. Lord, forgive me for harboring anger in my heart toward Jim, and forgive me for being angry at my mother. And Lord, forgive me for being angry with You." The instructor had said that once we confessed our sins, we were to take the paper, tear it into shreds, and flush it down the commode. It's a miracle my commode didn't back up that night. I had a lot of flushing to do!

After I flushed my paper down the commode, I opened to the back of the booklet and prayed the prayer I found there: "Lord, fill me with Your Holy Spirit." Absolutely nothing happened—until I woke up the next morning. I was a completely new person; all the baggage of twenty years had been lifted from my shoulders, and I was filled with such joy and love!

I was filled with such a hunger for God's Word that it was like a being a brand-new person. In fact, I went through several months of questioning if I had ever truly been born again because I did not understand what had happened to me. All of the verses I had learned in vacation Bible school now came back into my memory because as a child I had only memorized them to win prizes. Now the verses meant something to me. Likewise, all the choruses I had learned through the years became meaningful to me. In church, where we only sang from our hymnbooks, I found myself looking at those dry old hymns and thinking, *Wow! I didn't even know this was here.* I knew those hymns, every one of the sixth and tenth stanzas, by heart. But now they moved me—songs like "Amazing Grace." I found myself sitting in the congregation with my hands rising into worship and we didn't do that in our church. One Sunday morning the pastor actually stopped the service and said, "June, do you have a question?" From then on, I sat on my hands.

Once I was baptized with the Holy Spirit, I became a zealous Christian. I can't tell you how many people I assaulted with the *Four Spiritual Laws*, and how many people probably prayed the sinner's prayer just to get me out of their hair. You see, I was an Avon lady and I had my foot in the door of every neighbor's house. I would load my basket full of samples, catalogs, and my *Four Spiritual Laws* booklets, and I would go from door to door.

I was beginning to recognize the voice of the Holy Spirit and He began nudging me to share the gospel with the mother of five children who were the holy terrors of the neighborhood. I kept arguing with the Lord, "I don't want to go there." Eventually I couldn't handle it anymore. I said, "Lord, I give up. I'll go." I loaded my basket with supplies, including the *Four Spiritual Laws*, and I knocked on her door. I got all the way through my sales presentation, made a wonderful sale, then whipped out the booklet, read all the way to the back, and said, "Would you like to receive Jesus as your Savior and pray this prayer?" She looked me straight in the eyes and said, "No." I silently prayed, "Lord, I'm outta' here. I've done what You told me. That's all I'm required to do. Now You take care of the rest."

The very next Sunday I walked into our little church, where the same fifty people had worshiped year after year, and seated in the very back row right up against the wall were all seven members of that family. It happened to be the Sunday when the sermon was "You must be born again." On the tenth chorus of "Just As I Am, Without One Plea," all seven of them got up, made their way to the front of the sanctuary, and gave their hearts and lives to Jesus Christ. I thought my pastor was going to have a major heart attack. He had never seen that many people get born again. It was a day of rejoicing for them and for us.

Because of the drastic change in my life, my husband did not know what had happened to this woman who was living in his home. One night about three months after I had been baptized with the Holy Spirit, I woke up and he was sobbing into his pillow. I said, "Jim! Are you okay? Are you crying?" He said, "No. Not me." So, like a good wife, I reached up and lovingly patted him on the face. (I was checking for tears.) He later told me that he had prayed, "Lord, I don't know what You've done to June, but whatever it is she's got, I want it too." A week later he also was baptized with the Holy Spirit.

Our lives have never been the same. We have had one adventure after another. We raised two children who are walking with the Lord, and they have blessed us with five grandchildren. We've grown deeper and deeper in love with Jesus Christ and have served in ministry together for thirty-seven years.

A man named A. C. Dickson said, "When we rely on education, we get what education can do. When we rely on eloquence, we get what eloquence can do. When we rely on psychology, we get what psychology can do. But when we rely on the Holy Spirit, we get what God can do." [5] For twenty years I had relied on those things. What a waste! All those years I had spent working and serving in the power and energy of my flesh. Jesus said that anything we do in the energy of our flesh will not have eternal value. Certainly the people we're serving are blessed, but such work is not credited to our eternal accounts.

I had the privilege a few years ago of going to Niagara Falls. It was absolutely incredible. Everywhere I looked, people were wearing yellow rain slickers and galoshes, and they had their umbrellas open because the atmosphere was saturated with moisture. The buildings were covered with moss and everything was slippery and wet. I looked at the torrent of water rushing over the falls, and I thought, *Lord, this is exactly what You meant when You said out of our innermost being would flow torrents of living water.* Because it never dries up; it never diminishes; it never stops. When we are filled to overflowing with these torrents of living water, we can't help but touch the lives of those around us.

The need to be filled to overflowing with the Holy Spirit is not unique to me. In Ephesians 5:18, Paul exhorts each of us to be filled with the Holy Spirit. This is not an option but a command. In Acts 1:8, we are told that we *shall* be His witnesses when the Holy Spirit comes upon us. In John 14:16–17 Jesus told His disciples that when the Holy Spirit would come, He would be with us and in us, but there is this third work of the Spirit, in which He comes upon us. His desire is that we no longer remain a container for His Spirit, but that we become a channel for His life to flow from us to others.

You too can have torrents of living water flowing from your life by simply asking Him to baptize you with His Holy Spirit (Luke 11:11–13). Your life will never be the same!

Biography

June Hesterly has been married for forty-eight years. She is the mother of two married children and grandmother to five incredible grandchildren. She and her husband, Jim, planted and pastored a church in the San Diego area before returning to Calvary Chapel of Costa Mesa several years ago. June is a retreat and conference speaker and also serves on the Joyful Life Bible study board at Calvary Chapel of Costa Mesa. She has traveled throughout the world with Jim, director of Acts 1:8 Ministry, speaking about the gifts of the Holy Spirit, among other topics. They have co-authored three study guides for Pastor Chuck Smith's books, along with a pamphlet on the power of the Holy Spirit. June is also the author of a retreat planning guide.

Karyn Johnson

From Fear to Faith

*"Stand at the crossroads and look; ask for the ancient
paths, ask where the good way is, and walk in it,
and you will find rest for your souls."*
Jeremiah 6:16, NIV

Ever since I was a young child, I have always been very aware of the fact that I have the ability to choose between right and wrong. Deuteronomy 30:15 says, *See, I have set before you today life and good, death and evil.* Life is a continual walk of making choices—choices that lead to good in life or to pain and evil. Jeremiah 6:16 puts it this way: *Stand at the crossroads and look; ask for the ancient paths, ask where the good way is, and walk in it, and you will find rest for your souls* (NIV). We have the power, through Christ, to make good decisions, and God allows us to choose which way we will go. Looking back over my life, I am keenly aware of the fact that the Lord has always been incredibly faithful to me—even when I was making very bad choices.

I was born in Fort Worth, Texas, in the early 1950s. My parents were an odd mix and I never understood what drew them together. My mother had Masters' degrees in Music and English and my father was a construction worker who had never been to college. My father was from a wealthy Long Island, New York, family that had lost most of its money in the Great Depression. His family was secular, liberal, and highly involved in the Freemasons (my grandfather was a thirty-three-degree Mason). But my mother was a "P.K."—that is, a pastor's kid—and she grew up rather poor. Her father was a Brethren pastor and his parents were in lay ministry. Her mother was also a P.K.

My parents married during World War II when they were in their late twenties and they had problems having children for many years. My mom was forty when I was born. She was a schoolteacher who taught drama and music, so a nanny watched me during the day. Her name was Anna and I loved her very much. Our life in Texas, for the most part, was good. My mom was always exposing my brother, Rusty, and me to music, drama, and literature. She often brought instruments home from her music class, and we would have a lot of fun making noise and trying them out. However, neither of us ever learned to play a musical instrument.

I didn't meet my dad until I was four or five years old because he was working on the Baker Oil line in Saudi Arabia. He often sent us treasures— exotic things such as curved swords, ivory-inlaid boxes, and little rugs that I thought were flying carpets like the ones described in *The Arabian Nights*. Finally the day came to pick him up at the airport. My mother dressed me in a beautiful, white dress that floated on a layer of petticoats. The sky was bright blue, and as we drove across the tarmac, I watched the propellers of an airplane come to a stop. The door slowly opened and a man descended the steps of the airplane. Mom looked down at me and said, "That's your daddy." I felt no emotion for this stranger, but I recognized him from the pictures he had sent along with his gifts—mystical, magical pictures in which he was standing in front of a pyramid or the sphinx.

I had adventures of my own when we moved to Downey, California. We eventually settled into a tract of new homes in an area called "The Island." It was bordered on one side by a reservoir and on the other side by the Los Angeles River. Rusty and I would make rafts and swing from the trees and fall into the reservoir—just like the characters in *Tom Sawyer*.

My mother tried going to the local Baptist church, but hated the politics and soon left. Kenneth Taylor, a distant relative of ours, and the author of the *Living Bible*, gave me my first Bible. (It was called *The Bible for Little Eyes*.) But my greatest spiritual influence was a set of sixty sacred albums that my mom had bought. A free record player came with the albums. I would sit for hours listening to the old hymns and I would sing my heart out, even though many of the songs—such as "Rock-A My Soul in the Bosom of Abraham"—confused my immature mind. I learned all the words anyway. When I was sad, I would think back to the lyrics to songs like "Have Faith; Don't Cry." Peace would wash over me and I would feel close to the Lord. I had "some sort" of a relationship with the Lord as a young girl. I don't think I was born again, but when I did bad things, I was very aware of the fact that I was making wrong choices. And by the time I was ten years old, making bad choices—such as lying and ditching school—became a regular habit. (I got away with ditching school for the most part because both my parents were working, and in those days, written excuses weren't required until junior high.) I went to a Billy Graham crusade when I was twelve years old, but somehow I just didn't get it. I also had my first kiss when I was twelve years old, *and boy did I want more of that!*

The world was changing in the 1960s—with the Vietnam War, the Civil Rights movement, the Beatles, drinking, drugs, and hippies replacing the *Ozzie and Harriet* ideal of the 1950s. I wanted to be a part of all of it. But my make-believe world ended when I was fifteen years old. My boyfriend and I came upon a terrible accident right after it happened. My friend, Dave, was riding his motorcycle when he was hit by a drunk driver and thrown thirty feet into the air. He was killed instantly. I saw the crushed motorcycle and Dave's blood all over the sidewalk and I ran to his house. I knocked on the door and gave his unsuspecting father the news. He was a doctor and his wife had died of cancer the year before. The look of horror that came over his face was devastating. Dave was rich and talented. He had just graduated from a private, all-boys high school. And it was all gone in a split-second. His blood was cleaned off the sidewalk and people went on with life like nothing had happened.

Any innocence or purity that was left in me was destroyed by that one incident. I became cold and hard. I asked myself, *What is life all about anyway?* I lost my virginity the following weekend. Drugs and sex replaced carefree days of beach parties and surfing. This was a very dark time for me; I guess you could call it my "dark ages." My brother was drafted into the army and sent to Germany, and my mother was crying day and night, afraid he'd be sent to Vietnam. In the midst of this turmoil, I found out I was pregnant. I got so sick I had to quit school — just another disappointment in a long line of disappointments. Afraid to tell my mom, I went to my *pediatrician*. He called her the next day and told her that her little girl was going to have a baby. I'm sure she felt like she had lost both her children, and my father was little support for her during that time.

I loved the birth father of my baby and we talked of all the things that we could do, but we were very young and he only had a one-night-a-week job loading trucks. His brother was in Vietnam at the time, so his family was also in a lot of turmoil.

When I was five-and-a-half months pregnant, I was sent to the Florence Crittenton Home for unwed mothers in Los Angeles. I had never been away from home other than short trips to Baptist or YMCA camps. As one of fifty pregnant girls, I felt like I was just one of the herd in a big cattle factory. I hated being away from home and cried for the first month I was there. The social worker never talked to me about keeping my baby. She only spoke to me about adoption. *Anything,* I thought, *just let me go home.* If there was any color left in my life, it turned to black-and-white the day I gave birth to a beautiful, blue-eyed baby girl with velvet skin and thick blond hair. I never thought I would have a *daughter.* The nurse brought her to me the day after she was born. She was perfect. I took off all of her clothes to see this masterpiece. Oh, how I wanted to keep her!

The social worker came in that day with "the papers," but I just couldn't sign them. She was sent to a foster home and I was allowed to go home at last. I had named my daughter Natalie Elise. Natalie means "gift of Christmas." She was a gift, *but would she be mine?* A month-and-a-half later she was placed with her new family. I plunged deeper into depression, grief, and anger. From that point on I lived with a weight of grief that felt like one of those lead vests that technicians place on you when you have an x-ray. My boyfriend left for Hawaii and was later drafted and sent to Vietnam.

Two good friends of mine, Jeff and Debby, were also pregnant at this time. Debby had placed their son up for adoption about four months after I had given birth to Natalie. I had hid my pregnancy; however, everybody knew about theirs. But Jeff was also depressed about his son being given up for adoption. He would say, "How could a real mother do such a thing?" I knew I would never tell him about Natalie.

I had known Jeff since grade school, and although we had always been attracted to each other, we had never really dated. From the time we were in junior high he had told me, "Someday we'll get together. You're the kind of girl I'm going to marry." Now we started seeing each other every day. My mom said that when Jeff smiled it was like sunshine came into the room. She liked him more than all the other guys I had ever dated, which seems funny given his lifestyle.

Our friends took drugs for fun, but Jeff took drugs, mainly LSD, to find God. We would go to the Colorado River or down to the beach and Jeff would take heavy doses of LSD and scream at the sky, "God, where are You? Please find me!" I would look at our other friends, shake my head, and say "He's just stoned; he's out of his mind." But I understood at some level that he really was trying to find God. We dated on-and-off for six or seven months and then Jeff (like Natalie's birth-father) moved to Hawaii, where his life deteriorated into one long, drug-induced search for God.

My heart was set on being a nurse and I knew that I wouldn't be accepted into nursing school without a high school diploma, so I began going to night school twice-a-week. I took a job at a Taco Bell and one day while I was making tacos, I got very ill. It was a sickness that was all too familiar to me. I didn't need to take a test—I was seventeen years old and pregnant for the second time. I hid the pregnancy and learned to throw up very quietly. My heart was set on keeping this baby. I would make it on my own no matter what. I worked two jobs, went on welfare and Medi-Cal, and continued with school. My parents suspected that something was up, but they thought I was just becoming more responsible.

Jeff came home from Hawaii and within a few months Christina Lynn was born. Two months later we were married. My old boyfriend, Natalie's birth father, who had been listed as missing-in-action in Vietnam, came home on my wedding day. I wondered, *Why today?* This "coincidence" would haunt me for many years to come.

Married life was fun for about two months. Then one day as I was sweeping the kitchen floor and Jeff was sitting on the couch in the living room, I said to him, "This isn't fun anymore." He agreed, "Yeah, you're right. It's not." Jeff was working full-time and I was studying to be a nurse.

But Jeff was still on his God-search and was now taking opium. (I didn't take drugs after we were married because I had Christy to care for.) Our little house was a revolving door to various cults. Mormons and Jehovah Witnesses frequently came to talk to Jeff and he would have long conversations with them. But one day Jeff's opium supplier, Paul, came over. He had a very strange tale to tell. He had been in India buying opium when somehow the police were tipped off. Knowing that he was in danger, Paul told God that if He would get him out of the mess he was in, he would find Him and serve Him forever. Just as the police were coming into his hotel room, Paul found a heater vent that was loose and he hid the opium. He came home from India and heard about a little church in Costa Mesa. Remembering his promise to God, Paul went to Calvary Chapel that night and got saved. Now he was at our house, and instead of giving Jeff opium, he was telling him about Jesus Christ. Jeff accepted Christ into his life that same night. He flushed all of his drugs down the toilet and never touched them again. He stayed up all night reading the little *Good News for Modern Man* Bible that Paul had given him.

He began reading the Bible all the time and he seemed so different. I was stunned, but I was skeptical. Up until this point, Jeff was continually taking down my pictures of little country cottages and animals and replacing them with paisley tapestries and pictures of his gurus. He would replace my beautiful shag carpets with dark-colored oriental rugs and pile books about the cults he was studying on the coffee table. When I would come home from work, he would open the door and say, "Welcome to the chapel of the *guru-of-the-month*." I never knew who the guru-of-the-month was going to be. It could be Jesus, Paramahansa Yogananda, Krishna, or someone else. There would be incense burning and sitar music playing in the background. After I went to bed, he would stay up all night and chant "*om*" while standing on his head. I would have to beg him to stop so that he wouldn't wake the baby. But he would say, "I *have to* find God!" I felt so sorry for him, but his God-search had left me tired and angry. After nine months of marriage, I moved back home with my parents and filed for divorce.

Five months later, I was a divorced, nineteen-year-old single mother. I would look in the mirror and think, *Why am I such an old soul?* However, living at home with my parents was a relief. I felt like Dorothy coming home from Oz after a long and adventurous journey. My nursing program ended and I started a part-time job. But it wasn't long before new temptations were crawling toward me like snakes pursuing me across the lawn of my parents' house. My friend had a brother, the son of a wealthy Mormon family. He was a huge departure from any guy I had ever known and he wasn't caught up in religion or a search for God. His parents weren't thrilled about their young son dating a divorced woman with a baby, but he was completely enamored with me. His entire focus was *me* and I had never experienced that before. I ate it up like ice cream on a hot day!

> I was realizing what a lie the "free love" message had been. Love wasn't free! I had paid the ultimate price of sacrificing my firstborn daughter on the altar of "free love."

Jeff had moved into a Christian commune, the Philadelphia House, and I would see him from time to time. He would always tell me how much he was praying for me and how much he loved me and wanted his family back. I would literally laugh at him and say, "In your dreams!" He was attending Calvary Chapel of Costa Mesa every day. When the doors of the church were open, he was there. I had gone a few times, but the hippies were too much of a reminder of my "dark ages." However, when I saw Pastor Chuck Smith in his suit and tie, I thought, *If I were ever to get to the point of really going to church, I would listen to him.* He seemed closer to the religious roots of my mother than the young hippie pastor that many of the kids related to. Somehow I knew I wasn't running from Jeff and all of his weird ways—*I was running from God Himself.*

The Jesus Movement was in full bloom and my new boyfriend was even questioning his belief system. Soon he left for Hawaii. I thought, *Been there before!* I had moved into a seaside cottage for the summer and

100

many nights I would walk on the beach with my one-year-old daughter, Christy, and cry. I was so incredibly lonely, sad, and disappointed in myself because of all the bad choices I had made. I was realizing what a lie the "free love" message had been. Love wasn't free! I had paid the ultimate price of sacrificing my firstborn daughter on the altar of "free love." Christy was the recipient of my love for two daughters. I loved her more than anything in my life. I loved her for Natalie and I loved her for herself. I loved her "twice as much."

Summer ended and my boyfriend returned from his own God-search. I was in no mood to go through that again with another guy, so we broke up. I could feel the fall weather coming. It was time to go home. For the next year, I went on welfare and devoted all my time and energy to Christy.

Jeff and I started seeing each other again socially. He often told me about the baptism of the Holy Spirit. He would say that the Holy Spirit could give me power, but he would always emphasize "speaking in tongues." I had no interest in this weird-sounding supernatural stuff. (One day I actually made him speak in tongues into a tape recorder and I was going to take it to the language department at UCLA to have it analyzed to see if he was speaking a real language!) However, I was very attracted to the idea that the baptism of the Spirit might be able to give me power. I thought if I had power, I could make better choices. Because for me, life was all about choices.

One night, while I was alone in my bedroom, I prayed a very simple but sincere prayer: "Jesus, if You are really real, and You can help me with my life, give me direction, and help me with the stabbing pain of losing Natalie, please come into my life and fill me with Your Holy Spirit. I need Your power." What I felt, I can only describe as liquid sunshine splashing all over my face. This was no LSD trip; this was real. For days afterward I would wake up every day with the name of Jesus in my mind. I was truly saved and filled with the Spirit. However, I continued making some questionable choices. On New Year's Eve Jeff picked me up to go to church with him. But I wanted to go to a party. After a loud argument, he pulled the car into a liquor-store parking lot, and crying, he said, "Okay, okay! Let's just go to the party. What do you want? Beer, vodka, cigarettes, cigars? I'll buy anything you want." I started to cry as well. We went to church and welcomed the New Year by taking communion.

We were remarried by Pastor Chuck Smith at Calvary Chapel of Costa Mesa in May 1971, and soon our daughter, Tara, was on the way. Jeff began a Bible study in our home, but we quickly outgrew the space. The study was moved to a local church where Jeff became the youth pastor. He didn't want to leave Calvary Chapel of Costa Mesa, but with two children, the long drive was too much for us. When the Friday night youth study grew to be larger than the pastor's Sunday morning service, we were asked to leave. Pastor Chuck had counseled us to leave quietly and to take no one with us. He said we should not be part of a church division, so we went to a local park with two other families whom we had met in a restaurant, and New Life Fellowship was born. We had our first service in June 1973. It included six adults and six children.

Several months later, with winter on the way, we rented a small storefront for one hundred and fifty dollars a month. Pastor Chuck had challenged us to take a step of faith for the rent, saying that God would provide. As we were cleaning out our new three-room church, a man walked in the door. "What's going on here?" he asked. We told him what we were doing and then he gave Jeff two hundred dollars in cash. We had the next month's rent and the fifty dollars we needed to pay a cleaning fee! Jeff was never surprised when God provided, but I always was.

One night we showed the movie, *Gospel Road*, by Johnny Cash. We had invited everybody in town and anyone on the street who wanted to come. I invited my brother, Rusty, who wasn't saved at the time. After the movie, Jeff preached a powerful message that ended with the statement, "Don't leave this place without Christ. You could walk out and fall dead on the sidewalk. Ask Christ into your life tonight." When he was done speaking, we served coffee and cookies. Suddenly someone shouted, "Call an ambulance. Now!" One of the kids who had come to the movie was lying on the sidewalk. Fear gripped all of our hearts. We found out later he had died of a brain aneurysm. (Rusty didn't get saved that night, but he is a Christian today.)

Our growing church, now called Calvary Chapel of Downey, was the talk of the town with its young, hippie, former drug-addict pastor who had no formal training. A few years after we had begun meeting, a woman who wanted to start a Women's Aglow fellowship in Downey asked for my help. I went to one of the local meetings. There were about thirty-five ladies there who came for dinner and a message.

I was asked to make the announcements at our first meeting in Downey. What happened that night in 1975 changed my life for ten years. I had a panic attack. More than three hundred women packed the audience. I thought, *This is a far cry from the Downey Children's Theatre.* (I had once participated in a children's workshop there and I had often been asked to speak publicly.) At first I thought I was experiencing stage fright, which I had never had in my life, but I soon realized that this was different. Within six months I was gripped with fear in most social settings. My heart would pound and I would feel like I was dying. I was later diagnosed with agoraphobia. One of the many counselors I went to for help asked me if I was hiding anything in my life. "No! No way," I lied. But I was thinking about Natalie, my "somewhere child," and was clinging to the verse that the Lord had given about her from Psalm 138:8: *The Lord will perfect that which concerneth me* (KJV).

After I had been suffering with agoraphobia for about four years, I told Jeff, "This is hopeless! I will never be a good wife to you, a good pastor's wife, or a good mother." I started having thoughts that maybe suicide could be an answer.

We took a trip to Israel that was the catalyst for another turn in my life. (It may sound funny that I could travel to Israel with agoraphobia, but my agoraphobia was very specific. I would have panic attacks around authority figures and in certain social groups, but I was okay around people I felt safe with.) At St. Anne's Church in Jerusalem, I met a woman whose eighteen-year-old niece was pregnant. She was staying at St. Anne's Maternity Home in Los Angeles. Being at a church with the same name in Jerusalem had made this woman think of her niece. It was her desire that her niece's baby be placed in a Christian home and she asked if I knew of a Christian family who wanted a baby. I did know a Christian couple who was unable to have children, so an adoption was arranged. When that baby boy was dedicated, another gal approached me. She was nine months pregnant and in desperate need of a family to adopt her baby. So I helped her. As word spread, I began getting more and more calls from girls in need of couples who wanted to adopt. The House of Ruth adoption ministry was born.

I could now help pregnant girls arrange open adoptions, which are so much more humane than what I went through. The symptoms of my agoraphobia began to fade as God spoke to my heart and said, "The needs of the girls are greater than your fear." I had been on the Calvary Chapel pastors' wives board since its inception and everyone knew that my contribution would either be "behind the scenes" or in the skits that allowed me to hide behind the characters I was playing. And then, one year, Kay Smith asked me if I would like to do a presentation about the House of Ruth at the annual retreat. She suggested a slide show that would allow me to speak in the dark from a microphone set up in the back of the room. One of the other pastors' wives protested, "She can't do that!" Kay wanted to nurture the potential she had seen in me, and she said, "Leave her alone. If she wants to speak from the back, she can speak from the back." I took baby steps from there. For example, I would conduct women's prayer meetings at church in a darkened room with a night-light. Step by step I came out of it.

I returned to school and ultimately earned a Bachelor's Degree in Psychology. My life seemed to be in a good place. And then my mother died very unexpectedly. The pain was all too familiar. I had lost my baby and now I had lost my mother. I felt that I had to find my daughter. One night, while on a surfing vacation with my husband in Mexico, I stayed up all night praying. I said, "God, if it is Your will, would You please grant me Your permission to find my daughter." I woke up in the morning with the thought that I should read Jesus's parable of the lost sheep in Luke 15. In it the shepherd leaves ninety-nine sheep to find one that is lost. I felt God was directly telling me to find my little, lost lamb. I ran upstairs wanting to tell Jeff that God had spoken to me, but he still didn't know about my daughter. He casually told me to sit down and watch Billy Graham on TV. George Beverly Shea was just getting up to sing. His song was about the ninety-nine sheep and the one that was lost. I was stunned. God *really had* spoken to me.

About three months later I had her name, address, and phone number in my hand. I had hired a search consultant and she had found her in the Los Angeles County area. Natalie was only thirteen years old at the time and I didn't act on the information that I had, but instead prayed for God to let me know when the time was right to contact her.

During another trip to Mexico, I knew the time had come to tell Jeff and the girls about Natalie. I took Christy for a long walk on the beach. I wrote Christy's and Tara's names in the sand, and then I wrote Natalie's name above theirs. Christy asked me, "Who's Natalie?" I said, "She's your older sister." Her answer gave me chills: "Mom, I always knew there was something because you always loved me *twice as much*." I had never said those words to her!

I went into the camper where Jeff was chopping onions and said "Jeff, I have something I need to tell you." He said okay, and I broke down and told him my secret. Suddenly everything made sense to him: The many tears he had watched me cry over the years, never knowing what they were for; the birthday cakes I would always bake around Christmastime; and the pictures I would buy for our home that always included three little girls instead of two. "Karyn," he said, "I can't believe it was just a baby. I thought maybe you had murdered someone or you had been a homosexual before we got married." I couldn't believe that he would have forgiven me for being a murderer or a homosexual. At that moment, the monster—that lying monster that I had been feeding for so many years—died. I told Tara a few months later. Both girls couldn't wait to meet their sister.

A few years after we found Natalie, we found Jeff's son, Jeffrey. However, we waited for God to give us further orders on how to contact our little lost lambs. When Natalie was seventeen-and-a-half years old, I received a call at work from her adoptive mother. She said Natalie wanted to meet me and her sisters. What a blessing! The following night we spoke on the phone for two hours. She had been raised in a Christian home and her mom listened to Jeff on the radio every day. About a month after our first conversation, her parents invited me to come to their home to meet Natalie and to see the home where she had been raised. I gave her three gifts the day I met her: a big bouquet of her favorite flowers, a birthstone ring that I had bought for her on her sixteenth birthday (it was in the shape of a tear because I wanted her to know that I had shed many tears for her), and a homemade Cabbage Patch doll that my friend, Gail Mays, had made for her.

When I walked into their house, Natalie gave me a big hug. I was thrilled. I had prayed for this moment for so long. My baby had grown into a beautiful young woman. We shared pictures and stories about our lives. She asked about Christy and Tara and told me that when she would think about me, she always envisioned me with two daughters. She took me on a tour of her hometown, showing me her school, the parks that she had played in, and where she worked. It was wonderful day.

About one year later, Natalie was on a plane to Israel with my family. Although I had seen my three girls together, the first time I looked through a camera and took a picture of them, I was overwhelmed with a sense of God's incredible faithfulness. That Scripture I had clung to in those hopeless days of not knowing where Natalie was had come true: God had been faithful to *perfect that which concerneth me*. He hadn't make it good; He hadn't made it better; He had made it perfect!

The Lord has been faithful not just in my personal life, but in ministry as well. Looking back over thirty-two years of ministry, I see God's incredible faithfulness in answering prayer. He never leaves or forsakes, and without Him, we cannot do anything. Jeff and I grew up in Downey and we stayed in our hometown because Jeff has a burden for the Los Angeles area, which has gone through some real changes. Downey is one of the most densely populated cities in California. We have every culture at our church, even a few ex-Russian Molicans and Quakers, and we have the opportunity to share Jesus with all of them.

Jesus said He is the only way to heaven. Narrow—yes; exclusive—yes. Years ago Tara was lost in the middle of Los Angeles. Her frantic call was calmed by my very "narrow and exclusive directions" to get home. A loving mother wouldn't say, "There are many roads to home; *hope you find one*," and neither does God. There's one way, His way, through Christ.

Biography

Karyn Johnson has served alongside her husband, Jeff Johnson, senior pastor of Calvary Chapel of Downey, California, for thirty-two years. Ten thousand people attend Calvary Chapel of Downey, and 1,200 students attend the church's K–12 school. Thirty thousand people attend the church's annual Freedom Celebration held each Fourth of July. Jeff can be heard daily on the *Sound Doctrine* radio program, which airs throughout the United States.

Karyn is founder and director of the House of Ruth adoption ministry and of Calvary Chapel of Downey's women's ministry. Her passion is to equip women to put the needs of others before their own. Karyn and Jeff have raised two children and are reunited with the two who were given up for adoption. They have nine grandchildren.

Cathe Laurie

Living on the Edge

And for me, that utterance may be given to me,
that I may open my mouth boldly to make known
the mystery of the gospel.
Ephesians 6:19

I have always enjoyed a good mystery. Maybe because from a very early age, when I had profound questions about God, my mother would say, "Honey, it's a mystery." God was vast, distant, and, unknowable. So, I simply filed my questions about Him neatly into a compartment labeled *Mystery*. I would wait for further information.

The sisters at the Assumption Convent taught me to view my soul as a delicate, unseen, pristine-white object. Every time I broke a commandment, a black spot would appear on my soul that God could see. This was a very serious matter. Of course I knew that murder, idolatry, and adultery are sins. *The souls of really bad people must be completely black*, I thought. But then, selfishness, little white lies, and even laziness are sins as well. I wondered, *What does my soul look like?*

Sitting on the grassy lawn under the shade of the palm trees at our home in Quezon City, Manila, when I was about five years old, I overheard a conversation my mother and her friends were having about the "age of accountability." They probably thought I was too young to grasp what they were talking about, but I was listening. My interest was aroused because I had never heard this mysterious phrase: the age of accountability. At some point in the conversation it became clear that there would come a time in my life when I would be held accountable to God for the things I did. The discussion went back and forth until the grown-ups agreed it was sometime around the "magical" age of seven. Of course, there is no magical age, but I distinctly remember feeling like I was off the hook. *Whoo hoo! Lucky me. I've got two more years! But then . . . ?*

I was instructed in catechism class that through confession and penance my soul could be made white again. In preparation for my First Holy Communion, I pulled aside the heavy curtain door and entered the dark confessional. I was frightened by the sound of the small, metal-grated window sliding open from the other side. I knelt down and prayed, "Bless me, Father, for I have sinned. This is my first confession. . . ." After I confessed my sins, I was given absolution by the priest. I was relieved that it was over. I was forgiven and my soul was white again. *It is a mystery. Now do what you are taught and you should be good for a month or so*, I told myself. I exited the small confessional booth and returned to a pew in the sanctuary to say the penance I had been given.

Most of my childhood, we lived in Southeast Asia. It was a fascinating multicultural environment where I observed many religions. Buddhist shrines—like miniature houses—adorned with bowls of food or flowers dotted the sides of the roads. Saffron-robed monks journeyed on pilgrimages from village to village. Hindu temples overflowed with women in brightly colored saris celebrating annual festivals. Loudspeakers broadcasted the Muslim call to prayer from the minarets. In all this diversity, I was raised in a devout Catholic home. Although my dad was a Protestant, he agreed to let my Spanish mother raise my four siblings and me in the Catholic Church.

The first seven years of my life were spent in the Philippines, where the population was predominantly Roman Catholic. Later, we moved to Bangkok for two years where I was exposed to Buddhism. For a short time, when my father worked in New York City, we lived in Princeton, New Jersey, and after two years there, we returned to Southeast Asia to live in Malaysia. I spent my higher grade school and junior high school years at the International School of Kuala Lumpur, Malaysia. Kuala Lumpur was truly a melting pot of cultures and religions — Islamic, Buddhist, and Hindu.

To remember a Catholic childhood in the 1950s and '60s is to remember a church that was big and confident with tens of millions of members. It made me feel good, as if I was a member of something superior. Others had their religions, but ours was better. I was taught to make the sign of the cross, to say grace before every meal, to go to church every Sunday, and to go to confession once a month. Raised a typical Catholic, I always experienced some degree of guilt over even the most minor transgressions. And God, well, He was far, far away — too busy running the universe and communing with saints and angels to bother with my questions. I went to church faithfully, though it was often difficult to appreciate the traditional Latin Mass. To a six- or seven-year-old, it was simply a foreign language. For me, Sundays were something special mostly because after Mass we would have family time lingering over a delicious chicken curry luncheon.

Practicing my faith was akin to learning to write properly in cursive, or reciting the multiplication table — necessary, but unfulfilling. When I was around ten-or-eleven years old, I began to lose interest in the mysterious element of the Mass. But then, there were always the unforgettable lessons from the lives of the saints. Some were even young children, like I was, and I tried to imagine what it would be like to have a "visitation" or a "vision." But the saints were set apart, loved by God, and blessed with special grace. They would actually hear God's voice and He would guide and direct their lives. I was envious of that privilege. My unanswered questions lingered: *Why can't I be one of them? Why would they alone be chosen? It is a mystery.*

What a sharp contrast they were to the religion that I saw. There were many rituals, but I didn't see anything special in the ordinary lives of those around me. When I heard these stories, I longed for something more, anything, to know I was close to God. But as I understood it, being close to God was something like being the teacher's pet. Teacher's pets were chosen for special tasks: to take attendance, clean the erasers, and lead the line out to the playground for lunch. *God must have His pets too*, I concluded.

During Mass, I would look at my mother's face, covered with her long, lace veil. With her eyes closed and her face tilted to one side, she looked so beautiful, as if she was *experiencing something*. Kneeling beside her I would do my best to imitate her. Wearing my veil like she did, kneeling like she did, holding the rosary beads in my hands, even tilting my face at the same angle she did. Time after time I would wait and then give up, *Hmmmm, I guess I'm not one of the chosen ones.*

I accepted that I was apparently not appointed to any special grace like Saint Theresa, the "Little Flower," who heard God's voice and had intimate conversations with Him. Nevertheless, perhaps I could manage a commitment on the level of the nuns at school. They wore perfect, creamy, white robes and elaborate starched headpieces called "wimples" so that not a wisp of their hair was seen. I loved the worn, wooden rosary beads that hung by their sides and the way their robes floated behind them as they walked through the halls—like Maria in *The Sound of Music*. They weren't like the saints captured in stained glass. They had tempers that would flare up and waistlines that proved they enjoyed a hearty meal. I thought, *I could manage to be a nun, to be "married to Jesus."*

Sometimes after dinner and my bath, I would put a towel over my head, tuck it behind my ears, and pin it in the back. I would look in the mirror and imagine myself as Sister Catherine from the convent. I would wear this towel around the house as if I were a nun wearing a little veil.

One night I climbed into bed between my mom and dad. I turned to my mom and said, "Mommy, I think I want to be a nun." As a Catholic, she was delighted. She turned to my father and gushed, "Honey, did you hear that? Cathe wants to be a nun!" I distinctly remember my dad answering matter-of-factly, "Give her time. She'll get over it."

I did get over it. Back to Mass, back to memorized prayers, back to confession. Why was it that every time I went to confession I was given the same penance? Three *Our Fathers*, three *Hail Mary's*, and three *Glory Be's*. And of course, the Act of Contrition: *"O my God, I am heartily sorry for having offended Thee, and I detest all my sins, known and unknown, not only because I dread the loss of heaven and dread the pains of hell. . . ."*

I could compare my faith to a nice piece of luggage I carried on Sundays—one that was usually locked and kept in a closet somewhere, and somehow I was never entrusted with the key. The answer to all my big questions about God was always: *It is a mystery.* I wanted to understand, and this answer didn't satisfy me. I know now that many things are a mystery. God isn't small enough to fit into our minds. But He has revealed the mystery of salvation in the simplicity of the gospel message—a message even a child can understand.

I wasn't alone in my search for answers. I was part of a generation that wanted answers. Peggy Noonan wrote a book called *Life, Liberty, and the Pursuit of Happiness* in which she said, "My generation, faced as it grew, with the choice between religious belief and existential despair, chose marijuana." [6] That's exactly what many of us did. We had all these profound questions and no satisfying answers so we chose—marijuana. This choice, for me, was really a pursuit of happiness.

In *Mere Christianity*, C. S. Lewis rightfully said, "A car is made to run on petrol, and it would not run properly on anything else. Now God designed the human machine to run on Himself. He Himself is the fuel our spirits were designed to burn, or the food our spirits were designed to feed on. There is no other. That is why it is just no good asking God to make us happy in our own way without bothering about religion. God cannot give us a happiness and peace apart from Himself, because it is not there." [7] If we want happiness, we must find our way to the source of happiness. It's in Him. But somewhere in the late '60s, my generation decided to search elsewhere, expecting to be happy and fulfilled by experiencing the very things we had been warned about: extramarital sex, drugs, and rock-and-roll. Romans 1:21 says, *Although they knew God, they did not glorify Him as God.* In my pursuit of happiness, I turned my back on God.

And in the summer of 1969 all that foolishness took shape for me. My childhood had gone on in a seemingly smooth, endless routine. I was comfortable and secure. And then, everything changed. My two older sisters had both been away at boarding school—my oldest sister, Mary, in the Philippines, and my second oldest sister, Dodie, in Switzerland. When they came home for the summer holidays that year, they had changed. They looked and acted differently—spending most of their time in their rooms with the doors closed listening to strange-sounding music. Like the doors to their rooms, the rest of the family had been closed out of their lives. It was as if they were having their own little party, *only we weren't invited.* I asked them, "What is wrong with you guys? You're acting so strange. What has happened to you?" It brought back memories of when I was much younger and they would lock me out of their rooms. My sisters, who were beautiful and smart, had become rebellious and angry.

As I pestered them with questions, they told me that they had been experimenting with a drug called marijuana. "Marijuana? What is that?" I asked. They said it had opened their eyes and had given them this amazing experience. (It was the late '60s and everyone seemed to be following the siren-song of the counterculture.) Mary and Dodie told me that getting high gave them a mystical sense of peace and awoke their senses—books were more interesting, food was tastier, and people were funnier. It sounded cool and I was fascinated. Gradually, I was being drawn in, returning to the idea of mystery, *Maybe it is possible to experience God after all . . . but this time on my terms.* Before long I was saying, "Let me try it, *please, just this one time!*" I was in elementary school when I took my first hit of marijuana.

At that point, I decided I could find my own way. Church seemed irrelevant. I wanted meaning, enlightenment, and a good time. *Who needs all the duty and rules?* I decided. I felt the mystical peace and expansion of my senses that my sisters had described. And yet, at the same time, a "darkness" was beginning to fall all around our family. Home life was soon marred by continual conflict

> Gradually, I was being drawn in, returning to the idea of mystery, *Maybe it is possible to experience God after all . . . but this time on my terms.* Before long I was saying, "Let me try it, *please, just this one time!*"

with my parents. They could do nothing right. Mealtimes, unless interrupted by arguments, were endured silently. Dad internalized his worries. He was very quiet and controlled. I think he hoped that we would somehow grow out of it on our own. Mom, in desperation, prodded, questioned, and lectured about God, about faith, and about all the things she saw that we were doing wrong. It went in one ear and out the other. We lost interest in our hobbies, in school, and in the family. We spent more and more time sitting in smoke-filled rooms having what we thought were deep philosophical discussions. We debated hidden meanings of Beatles lyrics: *What exactly did the Beatles mean when they sang, "I am he as you are he as you are me and we are all together . . . I am the eggman . . . I am the walrus . . .*"?

This was an unhappy, conflicted time for me. Sure, we had fun (sometimes) and it felt like we were on the inside track of something significant, but we were living dangerously. Although people of various religions peacefully coexisted in Kuala Lumpur, Malaysia is a strict Muslim country. Selling drugs was punishable by death and the punishment for possession was imprisonment. On a small scale we were guilty of both.

The further down this road I went, the more guilt-ridden and anxious I became. I wasn't one of those kids who could entirely block out the pain I was causing my parents. Every time I came home, I could see it in their eyes. Isaiah 59:8 describes life at this time: *The way of peace they know not; and there is no judgment in their goings: they have made them crooked paths* (KJV).

And yet, God had mercy on our family. He began to work in a most providential way in my father, the least religious of my parents. My father had decided to leave his employment with Standard Oil Company. The company had offered to transfer him back to New York City, but he decided he would resign from his job and begin a new profession. (I think about that now—what a difficult decision for a forty-year-old man with five children to support.) He decided we were going to move to Orange County, California.

Proverbs 21:1 says, *The king's heart is in the hand of the LORD, as the rivers of water: he turneth it whithersoever he will* (KJV). My father was being turned by the hand of God in order to save our souls. God had to move us out of the situation in Kuala Lumpur to get us to Orange County where the Jesus Movement was just starting. We packed our bags and my sisters carefully stashed hashish in our record player.

We found Orange County to be about as multicultural and interesting as white bread. I felt out of place. I was homesick. I missed the jungle. I missed our eclectic group of friends in the international community.

Something was missing and it had to be more than a place or community of friends. At my new school, everyone seemed to move in little cliques. There were the "socialites," the "low-riders," and the "surfers." I stood out in my Indian-printed skirts and batik peasant-blouses. I had been the new kid in school many times before, but I found it was much harder now that I was in junior high. With Mary in college and Dodie in high school, I looked forward to our nights and weekends together.

I made a new friend named Cindy. We liked the same music and she wore tie-dyed dresses over patched, worn jeans. We got high and went to see the Doors in Los Angeles, dropped LSD, and missed the entire concert. We often ditched school to spend our days in the park. We sat in her bedroom smoking pot with incense burning, music playing in the background, and her mother banging on the door and yelling at her. Her response was simply to curse and swear back at her mother. *So much for peace and love! This was fun?*

And though I would never have admitted it, I was getting bored with it all. One day that first spring in California, Mary came home and suggested, "There's going to be a free concert at the college tonight; let's go and just get out of the house." So Dodie, Mary, Cindy, and I arrived for the concert a little early, just as it was growing dark. Shaded under the big trees on the east lawn of the campus, we sat in a tight circle and passed a joint. In the distance I noticed three guys walking toward us. They looked cool enough—long hair, muslin shirts, sandals, and torn jeans. I assumed they were coming over to share our pot. But instead of sitting down, they stood outside our circle and started a conversation:

"Hey, you don't need that stuff," one of them declared.

I thought, *Why not? What else is there to do in this concrete paradise?*

He continued, "We used to get high, but we don't need to anymore. We found what we were looking for in a personal relationship with Jesus Christ."

Did I hear that right? I was confounded by their statements, especially regarding their beliefs. Augustine said that to look for God is to find Him. *Could this be the answer?* I wondered. In my hazy state of mind I began to laugh. Soon my laughter grew out of control. I thought, *This is the most ridiculous thing; I don't even know why I'm laughing.* And then, a light went on. As a child I had believed in Jesus. Later, I believed in anything, everything, except Christianity. But at that moment, I began to doubt myself. I thought, *What if they're right? What if what they are saying is really true? What if it really was Jesus all along and I am laughing at what is holy and pure? What if I am on my way to hell?* I looked up at them and said, "How do you know there is a God?" Their simple answer was all I needed to hear: "We know there is a God because He has changed our lives." I asked myself, *Can this be true? This guy standing here in blue jeans and a T-shirt is some kind of saint who has had a personal encounter with God?*

As it turned out, the rock concert that we thought we were going to wasn't an ordinary concert—it was a *Christian* rock concert. We followed them into the small student lounge where there were about twenty other students sitting on couches and on the floor. Cindy and I sat in the front near the small stage. The band came out resplendent with their electric guitars and sang—about Jesus. When the concert was over, a speaker stood up to the microphone. "There may be some of you here who want to know about a relationship with Jesus Christ. If you're interested, why don't you stand to your feet right now."

I had a puzzling feeling like someone was tugging on my sleeve throughout the evening. Sitting cross-legged on the floor, I hesitated for a moment. *Did he say, "Stand up"?* I held my breath and then I alone stood up. I couldn't see my sisters anywhere. I looked down at Cindy and mouthed, "Why won't you stand up?" Reluctantly, she rose to her feet. *What happens now?* I wondered. Then the speaker came down off the platform, explained the gospel to us, and we prayed to receive Christ. When I went home that night, I felt changed. Everything looked beautiful. I felt clean; forgiven; chosen. *All those black spots were erased*, I thought. *So this is what absolution feels like. I, too, am near to God's heart.* I was flooded with peace. The weight of guilt I had been feeling was suddenly lifted. In its place was this unbelievable lightness in my soul.

The next morning I woke up to a clear mind, clear thoughts, and a deep assurance of the love of God. I felt like one of those saints whom I had always heard about, like my mother when she would pray and her face would glow. I prayed about what to wear, about which way to walk to school, and about whom to talk to when I got there. My first class the next day was history. It was all so new, but I had to tell somebody! I tapped the guy sitting in front of me on the shoulder and whispered, "You won't believe what happened to me last night!" I was perplexed when I heard him casually say, "Oh yeah, I'm a Christian too." I thought, *Funny, if you were a Christian, why wouldn't you have told me about this sooner?*

The following Wednesday evening, the guys who had witnessed to us drove us to a service at Calvary Chapel in Costa Mesa. I marveled, *Look at all these people and look at their faces; they seem so full of joy and love.* The singing was unlike any church choir I had ever heard. And Lonnie Frisbee, who looked like a first-century prophet, preached with such simplicity and conviction that I went forward again at the invitation. Some of the pieces of the puzzle were still missing for me, but I felt at least the borders were coming together. As the service was ending, I was led to one of the Sunday school rooms, where we listened intently to Pastor Chuck Smith explain the gospel clearly and simply. Even now, it's difficult to put the experience into words, but it was as if I had found my way home at last.

My conversion was genuine; I couldn't deny that. But a person needs more than an experience to go forward in their walk with the Lord. Fellowship and teaching are vital to spiritual growth. Sadly, though, Cindy and my sisters had heard the same message preached, but their lives weren't impacted like mine. I went home from church that night determined to read through the Bible and understand it. But Calvary Chapel was a half-hour drive from home. (It might as well have been in another state.) It was next to impossible to find transportation to church, and most of the time I was left to make head and tails of what I read on my own.

That summer my mother and I had wonderful talks about Jesus. She could see the change that took place in me. But September came and I began my first year of high school. Daily my walk home from school with Cindy became an exercise in enduring temptation. Gradually, day after day, I grew weaker and weaker. I never stopped believing in Jesus. I just forgot Him. I didn't wake up one day and say, "God, I can't believe in You anymore." I even kept my Bible on my dressing table, but I quit reading it. Profound and beautiful as it was, the flame of an experience began to flicker and eventually went out. I desperately needed to be taught the Word of God and to be encouraged by other Christians. Neither occurred. The Christian life seemed too hard. I couldn't be good anymore.

From September through December, I slipped into what felt like a comfortable, familiar, warm, dark pool. I cast off any remaining convictions. It was a relief from the battle of trying to hold on. Eventually, I dismissed my conversion as a religious phase that had worn off. And yet, the whisper of truth, like a nagging doubt, remained. If it was a phase, it was one I couldn't forget. Such peace of mind and heart is undeniable. Maybe after a few more years of delicious wallowing in the world, I would straighten up. I heard myself saying to friends, "One of these days I'm going to stop doing this stuff." I was all of fifteen years old and I had had enough.

It was my birthday, January 30, and a beautiful Saturday. Some friends and I decided to go to Laguna Beach to celebrate. Santa Ana winds were blowing and it was clear and warm. The sun was shimmering over the Pacific, and yet, as I sat with my back leaning against the warm cliffs, I contemplated what had become of my dreams. My friend, Jeannie, and I separated from the rest of our group. We walked down the beach, but my mood turned melancholy. I began to talk to her about what had happened to me the previous spring, how it felt to be forgiven, to be near to God, to know such joy and peace. I told her how in time I slowly turned my back on it all. Then I said to her, "One of these days, I'm going to go back to all that. . . ." just like I had been saying to myself for a number of weeks. She asked, "Why would you wait for 'one of these days'?" I said, "I guess I don't really have a reason." Then she said, "Tell me what you did." I told her I had prayed a simple prayer, something like: "God, I'm sorry for everything I've done. Forgive me, Jesus, and please come into my life."

"Well," she said, "Can we do that right now?" Her words caught me off guard; I never expected to hear her say that. I didn't need to wait a moment longer, "Do you want to pray with me, right here, right now?" I asked excitedly. Grabbing her hands, I bowed my head and led her in the same simple prayer I had prayed. When I looked up, my eyes met hers. We were both grinning from ear to ear and then spontaneously burst out laughing. I could see reflected in her face the same joy and peace I had known. How better to celebrate my fifteenth birthday than to recommit my life to Christ! It was under these unusual circumstances I had the privilege of leading my first person to Jesus.

It still amazes me to think back on that day. Two confused, young girls sitting alone on a beach, looking for answers to life and a relationship with God—in a moment, in a simple prayer—found God so near and ready to answer. Is it possible God could respond to such a prayer? Absolutely!

We began a walk with the Lord and with each other. We joined a group of Christians who met on our high school campus during lunch for Bible studies. And the most exciting thing happened. The Bible started to make sense to me. What a difference to know and understand God's Word and to have someone there to encourage me to do the right thing. As it says in Hebrews 10:24–25, *And let us consider one another in order to stir up love and good works, not forsaking the assembling of ourselves together, as is the manner of some, but exhorting one another, and so much the more as you see the Day approaching.* That is exactly what Jeannie did for me.

I was sixteen the first time I saw nineteen-year-old Greg. He was sitting on a stool with an open Bible on his knees talking about Jesus and Peter on the Sea of Galilee. We were in a coffee house filled with people sitting on couches or on the floor and he was teaching a Bible study. *What an amazing bundle of energy—cute, funny, and passionate for God,* I thought. He had a single focus: to love God and lead others to Christ. At times he made me laugh. At times he made me crazy! More than any other person, he helped me finally understand that following Jesus is not some ethereal experience; it is a daily discipline.

We became good friends. Soon we were going everywhere together. One day as we were driving home from a summer camp in the mountains, he turned to me and said, "I guess we're boyfriend and girlfriend now." It seemed like the natural next step, as there was a bond between us that I had never experienced with anyone else. But then he said, "I just want to make one thing perfectly clear, Cathe: Don't ever get between me and my relationship with Jesus. If you do, it's over." Great! What a refreshing contrast from previous boyfriends who had been too coddling, smothering, and accommodating. It was as if he was saying, "I'm headed in *this* direction and if you want to come along with me, then we can go together. But don't get in my way."

Don't get me wrong. We fought like cats and dogs and had a quarrelsome year or two of dating. People often see Greg as strong-willed and outspoken. They are right! But they are mistaken if they see me as quiet and compliant. There's a strong will underneath this quiet person. I didn't like being told what to do. I didn't like having someone else setting the course for my life. I had my own opinions and I wanted him to listen to me. So there was a struggle for control in our relationship until finally we looked at each other and said, "You know what? We're not going to be happy apart from each other. We just need to learn to get along."

We were married two days after my eighteenth birthday, much to my parents' dismay. At the moment I said, "I do," I became a *pastor's wife*. I had no idea what that meant for my future.

Fast forward thirty years: From my seat in the darkened auditorium on the first night of the 2005 Newcastle, Australia, Harvest Crusade, I reflect on all that God has brought me through. I wonder at the unsearchable grace of God, how He has been sufficient for every need. In a few moments my husband will share the message God has called him to bring to countless numbers—the message of the gospel. We were made by God and are loved by God. Until we realize this, we are never going to satisfy our deepest need.

I search the crowd, and amidst the blur of faces, I have no doubt some are searching for the meaning to their lives. Perhaps they've come out of curiosity, wondering what this American evangelist has to say. Many have probably come to hear the music. That's okay. After all, I did too, and that night my life was changed.

I pray for Greg and the message he will bring. *What a privilege to be a part of his life and ministry.* As I tuck into my seat among the crowd high in the bleachers, I notice the row of young girls in front of me and think, *Beautiful. Shiny hair in ponytails and braids, and oh my, jeans a little tight, skirts a little on the short side.* Welcome to a typical Harvest event. I ponder what brought them here this Saturday night.

It never fails to fascinate me. I play Sherlock Holmes, searching for clues as to what their stories might be. They look to be about in their mid-to-late teens. *They could be sisters, teasing, laughing, smiling at each other. No visible signs they are Christians.* For the moment, it takes me back to the student lounge so many years ago. *Is Something, Someone, tugging on their sleeve?* I close my eyes and pray, "Tonight, Jesus, let them fully discover how much You love them and the plan You have for their lives."

I can't take my eyes off of them. At the invitation one of the girls leans forward, elbows on her knees, face propped in her hands. She sits up, exchanges a look with her friend, and hesitates. And then, she stands up, grabs the hand of her friend, and pulls her to her feet. Moments later, the entire row follows her lead and makes its way down the stairs to the floor, weaving through the growing crowd in front of the platform. My eyes follow the girls until they disappear into the mass of people. I swallow hard and blink back the tears. *Jesus, for this purpose, this miracle, I am eternally grateful.*

As I look back to my earliest years I realize that the secret wish to be chosen to be a "saint" or a nun and to give my life to God was a God-given desire. I'm not a nun, but I am married to a man who is called to serve God, and I am too. I smile at the memory of Greg's words to me thirty-three years ago: "I am headed in the direction God has for my life, and if you want to come along, we can go together." I wanted to follow him then, and *I want to now.* Together we have a place in the kingdom and a place of service that is beyond our wildest dreams. I haven't always understood this mystery—God's desire to use human beings. I haven't always understood, in the moment, His working in my life, but I have understood enough. And I am satisfied because I know the story isn't finished yet. After all, I confess, I still enjoy a good mystery.

(When I give my testimony, I am frequently asked what happened to my sisters and friends. Mary and Dodie committed their lives to Christ shortly after I recommitted mine, and all five of us Martin children are believers. Ten years ago, my father converted to Catholicism. My friend Cindy dropped out of high school during her senior year. In our last conversation, I pleaded with her to stop abusing drugs and give her life to the Lord. She looked at me blankly, said it was good to see me, then turned and walked away. Tragically, about a year later, when she was nineteen years old, she died of a heroin overdose. My good friend, Jeannie, was still walking with the Lord the last time I talked to her.)

Biography

Cathe Laurie was born in Long Beach, California, and grew up primarily in Southeast Asia. She serves alongside her husband, Greg Laurie, pastor of 17,000-member Harvest Christian Fellowship in Riverside, California. Cathe has been a pastor's wife for thirty-two years and oversees Harvest's women's ministry, which reaches 2,000 women. Cathe and Greg have two sons, Christopher (31) and Jonathan (20).

Sandy MacIntosh

Twice Wed

"Behold, I make all things new."
Revelation 21:5

Home alone with my baby one night I heard a terrible banging noise. The phone started to ring. I picked it up and heard my neighbor's voice on the line. He warned, "Sandy, don't come out of your house! There's a man beating on your front door with a crow bar. Just stay where you are! We have called the police." They scared him away, and as he drove off, they wrote down his license plate number. My husband, Mike, eventually showed up, and a police officer took us outside to look at the door. He said, "The man who beat this door in is a notorious drug dealer here in Southern California." I walked back into the house and thought, *Where* am I? What has happened to my life? What has happened to my dreams? What has happened to my plans? I have no future. I have no hope. I was too ashamed to tell my family or friends how serious the situation in my marriage had become. How did I get here?

If you had asked me about my future when I was a young woman, I could have told you where I was going and what I wanted. I was raised in a family of overachievers. My mother's father was the first of the overachievers, and he set the bar high. He was Secretary of Agriculture in South Dakota and a friend of several presidents. He was an amazing man—a poet and a diplomat. My father was just as admirable. He emigrated from England, put himself through college, became a chemist, and later became the president of an international corporation. He was a very intelligent, well-read, sweet, sensitive man. My mother was a teacher, a dancer, an opera buff, a gourmet cook, and the consummate charity worker. She did everything with excellence. Before my father came home from work in the evening, my mother would actually change into a dress and redo her hair and makeup so that she would look perfect for him. My brother followed in their footsteps and is a successful attorney in Orange County, California.

I didn't fall into line with my family, but I wanted so much to be like them, and I was really proud to belong to a beautiful, all-American family. Growing up, I was a "good girl." I obeyed my parents. I took piano lessons, dance lessons, and classes in how to become a lady—learning to walk and talk properly and how to conduct myself socially. These things were very important to my family, and they became important to me. But I was also a product of this wonderful love in which I was cared for and protected.

I was turning out pretty much the way my family had envisioned. I went to college and studied diligently, but the deepest desire of my heart was to be a wife and mother. I wanted to be loved and I wanted to love. I wanted to have children to care for and a man to take care of me the way I had watched my father take care of my mother. My hopes and dreams were good, and I was about the business of pursuing them. When I came to Southern California from the Midwest as a twenty-year-old, I got a job at Disneyland and continued my education, just as I had planned.

And then, one beautiful spring day, I took a turn in the road that changed my life forever. I met a guy. (Isn't it so often a guy?) His name was Mike MacIntosh, and he was unlike any boy I had ever known. I had never brought home a boy like Mike. He had grown up with none of the advantages that I had had. He had no plan. He didn't know where he was going, and he didn't care. He didn't even know where he had been. He told me an incredible pack of lies: He said he was in medical school when he had actually dropped out of high school. He said he was a well-known musician, but I knew he could only play three chords on his guitar. He was immoral and incorrigible. But he was handsome, charming, and funny, and I was captivated. I was going to be his salvation. I would lead him onto my path, and where I was going, he would go too. He had come from a broken home and had an incredibly deep need to be loved. He needed an education; he needed a place to live; he needed a job; and, he needed a car. When I met him, he was earning money by playing the harmonica on a street corner and collecting pop bottles on the beach. I was so taken with him, and yet, to this day I do not know why. All I can say is that I really believed that with my love, my background, my education, and my family heritage, I could make him whole.

Exactly three weeks after I met Mike, I found myself standing in front of a justice of the peace in Las Vegas. As the ceremony began, I thought to myself, *How will this read in my hometown paper?* "The bride was barefoot; she wore a pair of jeans and an old T-shirt with a hole in it. The groom was dressed even worse." When we stepped over the threshold of the justice of the peace's office, reality hit me like a ton of bricks. I thought to myself, *What in the world have I done? Who is this guy? And how will I ever tell my parents?* The whole experience was surreal.

Afterward, we went back to Balboa Island where I had been sharing an apartment with friends. I withdrew my college tuition money from the bank and rented us a little house. So we had my place to live and my car, but I hadn't yet figured out that something was terribly wrong with this picture. I got a job as a waitress at a restaurant that was located on a paddle boat in the bay. On my third day of work, I rushed to the window to see my new darling, adorable, very tan husband paddling by on his surfboard. I said to the waitress next to me, "There he is! Isn't he just the cutest thing you've ever seen?" With a whole lot more insight than I had at that moment, she said, "Why are you in here and he's out there? I don't get it." I didn't get it either.

After we had been married a few days, I reluctantly called my parents. My mother answered the phone and was so shocked at what I had done that she refused to tell my father. She couldn't bear to hurt him and said I had to tell him myself. I called him while he was on a business trip. When he heard my voice on the phone, he tenderly answered as he always did: "Hi cutie!" Then, realizing something was terribly wrong, he said, "What's the matter?" Heartsick, I replied, "Oh daddy, I have done something really dumb. I have run away and gotten married." "To whom?" he asked. I explained that I had met a guy and had fallen in love. I said, "He never had a dad like you or a mom like Mom, and I think I can help him. . . . He really needs us, and I know I can make this work."

There was a long silence, and then he said, "From the moment I first held you in my arms, I've dreamed of the day I would walk you down the aisle on my arm, and my heart just broke into a million pieces." But my parents, troopers that they were, got on an airplane and flew to California to meet their new son-in-law. My mother brought two place settings of china and sterling silver utensils. She thought that made everything okay.

When my parents met Mike, I could see by the way they were looking at him that they were wondering, *How could she have done this?* However, they were determined to be supportive. They asked my husband questions that fathers ask a boy who comes to pick up their daughter for a first date: "What are your plans?" and "What would you like to be when you grow up?" Much to my surprise, Mike said, "I've always wanted to be a pilot." I don't think he had ever been on an airplane. He'd been hitchhiking around the United States. But my sweet father decided that if this husband of his only daughter wanted to be a pilot, then he would certainly help him to achieve his dream. Daddy bought Mike an airplane and Mike took flying lessons.

After a few months, I realized that there was much more to this man than I had ever imagined. There was trouble worse than I had ever seen. Mike was searching for God and he thought he could find Him by taking drugs. This was a time in our nation's history when drugs were not prevalent like they are today. Young people were just beginning to experiment with them. I had married this kid who was so wretched, so lonely, so lost, and so confused about himself and about life that he actually thought he would find meaning in drugs. But I knew nothing about drugs. I certainly didn't know he was involved in that world. I didn't know that our garage was full of drugs. And I didn't know that most of the time when he was out, he was taking really dangerous mind-altering and mind-destroying drugs. I didn't know how really lost he was.

As I began to realize how bad the situation really was, I desperately tried to figure out how to make my marriage work. You see, there is no divorce in my family. There is really no failure at all, except for me, and I was determined that no one would know what was going on. I was determined to make it work so that my family would be proud of me. I decided that what we really needed was a home of our own. I talked to my dad, and as my dad was inclined to do, he bought us a house. So now we had an airplane and a house and not much else. Neither of these things provoked change, so I decided that what this guy needed was the family he had never had. I got pregnant. This may sound like a stupid plan, but I was young and desperate. Nine months later I gave birth to a darling, adorable little girl.

Things went from bad to worse. Mike hardly ever came home anymore and his drug problem worsened and became more dangerous. After the incident with the drug dealer trying to break into our house, Mike made several attempts to make things work. He got very involved in Eastern religion and set up a big statue of Buddha in our living room. We went to Los Angeles to learn how to do transcendental meditation. He tried to get me involved in drugs, but they were abhorrent to me. Every day he slipped further and further away. He wasn't really living at home anymore, but he would show up at our house after the bars closed at about 2:30 a.m. During one of those visits, I got pregnant. So now I had a nine-month-old baby, another one on the way, and an absentee husband. I had no money, but I still couldn't bring myself to tell my parents what was going on. I went to Mike and pleaded, "You have to get your life together and take responsibility for this family. You have to get a job and stop what you're doing." Angrily I said, "My plan was to have a wonderful family and you have ruined my plan. You have ruined my life and my future. You have ruined my children. You've ruined everything!"

> Finally I looked at him and asked, "Don't you love me?" because in my mind love fixed everything. He could barely focus his gaze on me, but he looked at me and said, "I love everybody."

I felt so stupid. By then he didn't even look like he used to look. His hair was down past his shoulders, his eyes were glazed over most of the time, and he weighed practically nothing. Finally I looked at him and asked, "Don't you love me?" because in my mind love fixed everything. He could barely focus his gaze on me, but he looked at me and said, "I love everybody." I don't know why, but that is what it took for me to give up. I walked to my garage, took off my wedding ring, and threw it into the garbage can. And then I called my parents and said, "I'm in trouble; bring me home."

In twenty-four hours I was packed and on my way to their home in Philadelphia. Our house was put up for sale and I never, ever wanted to see Mike again. He was my big shining failure. To me that meant my love was good for nothing. I felt so humiliated. I kept asking myself, *Where am I?* My parents didn't think I should get a divorce while I was pregnant, which was probably a good idea. While I was having our baby on the East Coast, my husband moved into a house in Laguna Beach where he and a group of people took drugs twenty-four hours a day. He mixed all kinds of chemicals together, trying to find meaning and purpose, and searching for God. He would write me absolutely ludicrous letters full of lies and hallucinations. He had completely lost touch with reality. In one letter he said he had met the Beatles on Pacific Coast Highway and that they had written some songs together. He wrote nonsensical little poems to the children. It may sound funny, but reading those letters, I thought, *This is the communication I have to show his children?*

I was so destroyed. I didn't know what to do. I didn't know how to get help. I didn't know how to go on. But I came from this family of overachievers and so I was determined to somehow get my life together. After our second child was born, I moved back to Southern California and divorced Mike. With my parents' help, I enrolled at Cal State Long Beach and got a little apartment.

Soon after I moved in, Mike showed up at my door, only now he was a shell of a man. While I was in Philadelphia, he had badly overdosed on drugs and ended up in the Orange County Mental Hospital. I didn't want him to come into the apartment, but he just opened the door and walked in. He went straight to the back bedroom where our four-week-old baby boy was asleep in his crib. Mike had never seen him. He picked the baby up and held him. With tears streaming down his face, he brought him into the living room. I thought, *This is the only father that my children will ever know. What a tragedy. What a loss.* I wanted him to disappear.

Time went on and I got back onto what I thought was the right road, doing the things that I knew best how to do, trying to make a life for myself and my children. But always there was this shadow of a man lurking in my life and showing up at unexpected moments. He would stand at my front door, and looking at him through the screen, my heart would fill with pity for him, for me, and for my kids. He would come in, sit on the couch, and cry. He couldn't say a sentence with a subject and a verb.

Then one day about a year after I returned to California, there was a familiar knock on the door. Looking through the screen, I could tell that something was different. Mike came into the house and said, "What do you know about Jesus Christ?" This question infuriated me. I had gone to church my whole life and had sung in the choir from the time I was five years old. I had been confirmed. I certainly knew much more about Jesus Christ than he did. Angrily, I declared, "Oh, a whole lot more than you do!" Undeterred, he pressed on, "No, I don't mean what do you know *about* Jesus Christ. I mean *do you know Jesus Christ, Himself?*" I couldn't believe this guy was trying to tell me about God. I said, "You tried to get me into drugs, then you took me to a maharishi, and we had a Buddha in our living room. Now don't talk to me about religion. Get out of here!" He turned around and walked out. But he would not leave me alone. Every couple of days, he would be at the door again, asking, "Do you know Jesus Christ?" And I would say, "Go away. Leave me alone."

But the most amazing thing began to happen. I watched him get well. He began to speak in complete sentences and interact with his children. He told me the story of what had changed him. He said that his car had broken down in the parking lot of Calvary Chapel in Costa Mesa one day. He had gone inside to see what was going on, but nobody was there. A few days later some friends from Orange Coast College took him to a service at the church and upon hearing the gospel he gave his life to Jesus Christ.

The following Saturday he went to a men's prayer meeting where the men laid hands on him, and he was instantly healed of the brain damage he had suffered. As I watched him get well, I wondered, *What is this power that has done what my love was unable to do?*

One day he called me and said, "I'm not going to bug you and I'm not going to come over, but later this evening there is an event at the beach in Corona del Mar. If you want to see what I've been talking about, get a babysitter, go down there, and see for yourself."

Just so that he would stop bothering me, I got a babysitter, picked up my cousin, and went to the beach where there was Christian concert and a mass baptism taking place. It was a long walk from where I parked my car to the water's edge where people were standing in line to be baptized. With each step I took, I felt like I weighed a zillion pounds. And yet, I could almost hear someone on the beach beckoning me onward. I walked and I walked and as I got closer to this big group of people, I knew in an instant that I should get baptized too.

Other than the detour I had made with Mike, I was a woman who made decisions carefully. So it was out of character for me to walk up to this crowd of people and get in line to be baptized. Standing next to me was a big old surfer. He turned to me and said, "Are you going to get baptized?" I said, "I think so." "Are you saved?" he asked. I told him I wasn't sure. "Well, I've been saved now for three weeks so let me lead you in the sinner's prayer," he replied. There was no time to think, no time to question, and no time to figure it out. The line was moving and pretty soon it was going to be my turn. I bowed my head and asked the Lord to forgive my sins and save me. Before I knew it, I was in the water being baptized. When I emerged, I was instantly changed and filled with the Holy Spirit. I think God worked this way in my life because if He had given me five minutes to think about it, I would have said, "No thank you. That makes no sense at all. The plan of salvation is totally illogical."

I left the beach and drove straight to Mansion Messiah, a Christian commune where Mike was living. I knocked on the door, dripping wet, covered with sand, and glowing like a light bulb. When Mike opened the door, I said, "Okay, you were right about this one thing." I went home and he did his thing and I did mine. We went to church together, prayed for our kids together, and became friends. I was so excited about the things of the Lord that I could hardly stand it. I devoured my Bible. I was at church every single night. I dragged my kids with me to every concert and every fellowship. They grew up at Calvary Chapel in the Sunday school program and their teachers did a good job. I had finally figured out what I needed. I didn't need a husband or a family. I didn't need to be loved by a man. I didn't need the American dream. I didn't need an education or a plan. I needed a Savior! And once I had Him, I had everything I needed. I had a best friend. I had a lover of my soul. I had the One who had redeemed me, restored me, released me, renewed me, and captured my heart forever. I was so full of joy and hope. I developed new plans for my life and those plans did not include a romantic relationship with Mike. I was very happy he was doing so well. But there was no way in the world that I could imagine that we would ever be together again. Pretty soon, however, he started calling and telling me that he really felt that it was God's will for us to get remarried. I would say, "No, I'm pretty sure that that is not God's will. I am perfectly satisfied and happy." He would try to convince me, but I was adamant, "No, uh-uh, no way!"

And then, one day, I was driving to class at Cal State Long Beach. As I was driving, I was having a conversation with the Lord. I was saying, "Lord, You are so wonderful. I can't imagine how I ever lived without You. I know that it can't be Your will that I end up with this guy again. Being married to him was so painful." It was a conversation I had had many, many times with the Lord, and I had always believed He was in perfect agreement with me because He was always quiet. But, on this day, He did not choose to be quiet. There have only been two times when I have heard what I felt was the audible voice of God and this was one of them.

A very deep, authoritative voice spoke a Scripture to me that I didn't even know existed. It said, *Behold, I make all things new* (Revelation 21:5). Startled, I thought, *Whoa . . . is my radio on?* I pulled the car off the road, shut off the engine, and checked the radio. I was so new in the Lord, so fresh and eager, that I whispered, "Lord, are You talking to me? Do You actually speak out loud to people?" Again I heard a voice as clear and as authoritative as any I had ever heard in my life. It reminded me of my dad calling my name when I was a child. The voice said, *Behold, I make all things new.* That was all I needed. I turned the car around, went home, and called Mike. I said, "Okay, you're right again. God wants us to be married."

We waited a year to get remarried and it was awful to wait, but it was also good to wait because we had rushed into it the first time. Throughout that year the Lord turned my heart around. He gave me back the love I had felt for that young kid several years earlier. Before long I could hardly stay away from Mike and my heart would stop every time he called. (It still does to this day.) Finally our wedding day arrived. I stood at the back of Calvary Chapel and took the arm of my dad. Together we walked down the aisle to this guy who had tears running down his face and dripping off his chin onto his borrowed sport coat. He was crying so hard that he took my dad's arm instead of mine, and we stumbled up to where Pastor Chuck Smith was standing. It seemed that everyone was crying—except my mom and dad. They could not believe I was doing this again. Mike's mom refused to come to the wedding. She called me beforehand and said, "Are you stupid? You're really going to marry this guy again?" That was before they all came to know the Lord so they didn't understand.

As we walked out of the church with our little girl in front of us—she was the flower girl—and our two-year-old son waiting in the back, I thought, *What an extravagant God!* Have you ever considered the extravagance of

God? He doesn't mete out blessings in tiny little portions. Scripture says He "opens the windows of heaven and pours them out upon us" (see Malachi 3:10). He didn't put a couple hundred stars in the heavens for us to look at. He put millions of stars in the sky, some that we will never see. He is so extravagant that He created not just a few species of animals for us to enjoy, but He created countless varieties. He is incredibly extravagant in His love, mercy, and grace, and in His healing and restoration. He lavishes us with those gifts. On top of all that, He spared not His own Son for me so that I might have new life, so that I might have a future, a hope, and a family. All the things that I had always wanted were now mine.

Mike told a story one Sunday morning that illustrates my experience. There was a very wealthy man in England several hundred years ago who was much older than his only son. The mother had died in childbirth and he had raised the boy alone. When the man was in his seventies and the boy was thirteen years old, the man died. He had an enormous inheritance and his will directed that his estate be dispersed by auction. The whole community came to this auction. The first thing to be auctioned off was his son. The people were shocked and as the auctioneer called for bids there was no response. Finally a man said, "Okay, twelve pounds for the boy." There were no opposing bids so the auctioneer slammed down his gavel and declared, "Sold! The son is yours for twelve pounds. And now the auction is closed." The people were furious. They complained, "That's not fair. What is going on here? We have come with money to spend. How can this be?" The auctioneer said, "It is the will of the father that he who has the son gets everything." I was so overwhelmed that God would give me His Son, and once I had His Son, I had everything I had ever wanted or needed.

Mike and I went on to have three more children and Mike went into the ministry. I followed reluctantly behind him. I thought it was enough that God had saved him. The idea that God could use him was, in my estimation, beyond even God's realm of power. But this man who had dropped out of high school went back to school and earned three masters degrees and a doctorate. He has traveled the world preaching the gospel. Traveling with him and watching God work through him has been an incredible blessing. I have seen him lead thousands to Christ, and I have been privileged to watch him shepherd his flock and father his children in a way I would never have thought possible. His children all love and know the Lord. At this writing, we have sixteen grandchildren. However, God is never done transforming us into the image of His Son.

After Mike and I had been remarried for a number of years, an issue came up that gave me a chance to die to my dreams once again. It also brought the work of redemption to a conclusion in Mike's life. He had gotten his girlfriend pregnant when he was sixteen years old, but he had never seen his child. (He wasn't even certain his ex-girlfriend had given birth.) We decided it was time to find out what had happened to his child, and with the help of our friend, Karyn Johnson, we eventually discovered that Mike had a daughter named Joy. She had been adopted by missionaries. I was so privileged to listen to their first conversation and to hear that she had been a Christian longer than Mike had been. She had been looking for him, but she didn't even know his last name. They made plans for Mike to drive to her home in Palm Springs the next day so that they could meet. We filled his car with teddy bears to make up for all the years that he had missed with her. When it was time for him to leave, I walked out to the car with him to pray with him and say good-bye. He was so cute and nervous. He asked, "Do I look okay? Should I lose weight before I go?" I said, "Just go. She's going to love you."

He drove away and then I waited by the phone for approximately eight hours. I felt so left out and wondered what was going on. Finally the phone rang. "It's going great. You won't believe it," Mike said, "This is so wonderful. Here, I want you to talk to somebody. Say hello to my granddaughters." I thought, *Ohhhh! Not grandchildren! Not grandchildren!* Because my plan was that we would have our own grandchildren. In fact, our oldest daughter had just had a miscarriage. I thought, *This is not fair. He gets all this and I just wanted a grandchild of our own.* I had these romantic dreams of Mike and I at the hospital looking through the window of the nursery at our first grandchild. Once again, my plan was ruined. (After all God had done for me, can you believe that I was so stingy about this?)

When he arrived home that night I said, "I know you have these two grandchildren, but they're not my grandchildren. I'm waiting for my own grandchildren." I was very sweet and kind when they visited and they were darling, but they were not my grandchildren. Every time I heard them call Mike "Grandpa," it was like somebody put a sword in my heart. He carried them around on his shoulders and I thought I would die in agony—me to whom God had been so merciful. I said, "You have to tell the girls to call me Sandy; I don't want them to call me 'Grandma.' I'm waiting for my own grandchildren, and I will really never be their grandmother. So, you be their grandfather, and that's just fine."

Over time we developed a close relationship with Joy and her family. One day we got a call that she was about to deliver her third child. Mike and I drove to Palm Springs in order to be with her for the birth. He went to the hospital and I stayed in the hotel with the two girls. (They were three-and-five years old.) I thought to myself, *Great! Mike now has three grandchildren on his scoreboard and I've still got nothing on mine.* We waited a long time for the phone to ring, and the girls began to get cranky. I said to the little one, "Whitney, you need to lie down and take a little nap. I'll wake you up as soon as Grandpa calls, and then we'll go to the hospital to see the new baby." She stormed off and three minutes later she was back saying, "I don't want to be there by myself; you come too." "Okay," I said. So I lay down on the king-size bed with her, but I kept my distance because she was cranky and weepy and she was *not* my grandchild. Then she whined, "Not over theeere, over heeere!" I moved to the middle of the bed, but that still wasn't close enough for her. She suddenly threw herself on me and pressed her tiny face right up against mine. And then, as she was about to fall asleep, this outspoken little girl whispered in the tiniest, sweetest voice, "Sandy, when will you be ready to be my grandma?" I was so broken and humiliated before God, who had been so extravagant with me. I said, "Oh Whitney, I'm ready right now if you'll let me be your grandma." And I have been her grandma ever since.

What is it that you hold back from the Lord? Are you only giving God a tiny little portion of your life, your heart, your plans, or your ideas? My problem was that I was only willing to love Whitney as much as I thought I could. As I lay there on that bed, I thought, *I am so glad God didn't love me just "this much," but instead He held nothing back from me.* He has never failed me or left me. He is my rock and my fortress. He's my best friend. All He wanted to do was to break open my heart to show me my stinginess. Don't hold back from the Lord. Let Him have your whole life.

As a child, I memorized Psalm 23, but it didn't mean anything to me. Now it means a great deal to me. I have paraphrased it in my own words to sum up the testimony of what my gracious Savior has done in my life:

> For many years the Lord was not my Shepherd, and I lacked for everything.
> There were no green pastures; all the land was dry and barren around me.
> The waters of my life were tumultuous; they were treacherous and terrible.
> My soul was thirsty, restless, and lost.
> I traveled the path of sin and self for my own sake.
> I spent much time in the shadows and in the valley where I feared everything because God was far from me.
> I had no correction or comfort, and my enemies prepared me for their dinner.
> There was no anointing upon me; my cup was empty.
> Confusion and contention followed me everywhere, and I had no hope of eternal life.
> But now, I have a Shepherd. He is Creator. He is King of the universe. He is my Lord and Savior, Jesus Christ.
> Now I take naps in soft green pastures;

He stills the raging waters of my life, and we walk together beside
  them.
My soul and my spirit have been restored and healed by Him.
He leads me from my own path of sin and self down the paths of
  righteousness and holiness.
I am even called by His Son's name.
Life can still be difficult and scary, but I feel His presence and I am
  not afraid.
I have felt the discipline of His rod and the direction of His staff. He
  even broke my leg once so He could spend more time with me.
My enemies have remained, but with Him near, I am fed, I am safe,
  and I am loved. As long as I stay close to Him, goodness, kindness,
  and mercy flow from Him to me, forever and ever.
I have all that I need, and more than I ever dreamed.
Some day soon He will take me to His house forever.

Biography

Sandy MacIntosh surrendered her heart and life to Jesus Christ
over thirty years ago. She is the wife of Mike MacIntosh, a pastor
and evangelist with a vision to win people to Jesus Christ, disciple
them in Christ, and send them out for Christ. Mike is the pastor of
Horizon Christian Fellowship in San Diego, California. Over one
hundred churches and para-church organizations worldwide have
grown out of this congregation. Sandy has spoken evangelistically and
as an encouragement to pastors' wives and women across the United
States and the world. She currently teaches two weekly women's
Bible studies at Horizon. Sandy attended Stephen's College and
Cal State Long Beach.

Sandy and Mike live in San Diego and have five children and
sixteen grandchildren.

Gail Mays

From Flower Power to God Power

Therefore, if anyone is in Christ, he is a new creation;
old things have passed away;
behold, all things have become new.
2 Corinthians 5:17

To some people, the state of Indiana is best known for the Indianapolis Speedway, but to me, it is the quiet farm country where I spent my early childhood. I was born in South Bend and was raised in a Catholic home. Even though I attended church religiously and had been taught about God, I had never learned that I could have a personal relationship with Jesus Christ. My family moved to Southern California when I was only nine years old. Never a troublemaker, I did well in school. I was a good kid—the quiet type who always sat in the back of the classroom. Yet in spite of my good upbringing, I went astray as a teenager and became a totally different person.

The Vietnam War started in 1965, during my senior year of high school. Like so many young men, my high school sweetheart was drafted into the Army. Our plans to get married upon my graduation and live happily thereafter were put on hold until he completed his service abroad. You can imagine how brokenhearted I was to discover that when he returned, he was no longer interested in marriage. After two years of faithfully waiting for him to make my dreams come true, life, as I knew it, was over. I was devastated.

It was about this time that the infamous hippie movement began. My generation was searching for something meaningful to hold on to in an uncertain world. So was I. I quickly fell headfirst into a black hole of drugs, parties, love-in's, protest marches, loose morals, and rock concerts. I rebelled against everything my parents had taught me. Suddenly, at only 18, I was "hip" and my parents were "square." In my opinion, they did not know what life was all about, and obviously they couldn't do anything right! Unlike them, I was on my way to discovering Utopia. I was determined to experience what peace was really about, and I was going to discover true love.

Looking back, I realize that I was a child of the devil doing his bidding. I lived for concerts, dances, parties, boys, and drugs. LSD and its derivatives were my "thing." In fact, I thought hallucinatory drugs were wonderful. Drugs have such a way of distorting reality. They make the world look so inviting. While under the influence of drugs, people often believe that everyone is wonderful, that there is no right or wrong. I became known as a "flower child" associated with the comical slogan "flower power." The "flower philosophy" called us to renounce materialism, to live for the moment, and to always stop and smell the flowers. I wore flower wreaths in my hair. My wardrobe was very simple: a peasant blouse, bell-bottom jeans with an embroidered peace sign on the back pocket, open-toed sandals, and an occasional sweatshirt.

During this time, I became involved with a guy. It wasn't long before I found out I was pregnant. But things just weren't working out for us, so we chose to go our separate ways. This choice left me with the reality that I was single and about to have a baby. Prior to my pregnancy, I had held on to the ideal that my children would live in a loving and secure home with their mommy and daddy who loved each other. Knowing that I could not provide this type of environment for my unborn child, I decided to give my baby up for adoption. Abortion was never an option for me. It simply did not enter my mind.

On April 22, 1969, I gave birth to a beautiful but tiny baby girl at Queen of Angels Medical Center in Los Angeles, California. She weighed four pounds, two ounces and had blue eyes and blond hair. The only time I saw her was in the delivery room. In those days, babies who would be given up for adoption were taken away immediately after birth. People feared that if the birth mother held her baby, she would bond to her newborn and have difficulty letting go. The adoption agency wanted to make it as easy as possible for the birth mother, so I left the hospital empty-handed. I was told to get on with my life and to pretend that the pregnancy had never happened. I tried to do that for many, many years. It was so hard. My baby's newborn cry lived in my head for a very long time. I often cried myself to sleep, wondering if I had done the right thing. Sometimes I woke up in the middle of the night thinking that I had heard her cry. Was she crying for me? Did she need me? The mental torment was horrible. I prayed over and over again, "Dear God, please take care of her. Please give her a good home."

Even though I was not following the Lord, I was very God-conscious. I didn't understand that I was missing out on a personal relationship with Jesus. I was just doing what I thought was the right thing to do. Looking back, I can clearly see that God's hand was always upon my life. He was guiding me toward Him and moving me to a place at which I would make a commitment to follow Him. I am able to look back on my past and say, "Yes, God did have a plan for my life."

But still, for many years I felt terrible for what I had done. It was hard to ignore my feelings of guilt, shame, and condemnation. I had received a lot of counseling before the birth, but absolutely no counseling after it. This is very similar to what women who have an abortion face today.

> I said to Mom, "Where is that Calvary Chapel you've been talking about? You know, the place where kids go in their bib overalls and bare feet and the guys have long hair and beards? Where it's just like back in the days of Jesus and some guy with a bald head talks about God?"

There's often no counseling for them either. They are advised to get rid of their babies, and afterward they are left to agonize over what they have done.

I dealt with my guilt the only way I knew how. I descended deeper and deeper into the tragic fantasy world drugs created for me. After several years of selling and using drugs and thoroughly neglecting my body, the abuse took its toll on me. I became what you might consider "dingy" looking. I couldn't think straight anymore. I even had trouble making good drug deals, which resulted in a lack of money on which to live. The only choice I had was to ask my parents if I could move back home. My mother, who had grown weary of me moving in and out so many times, said, "No way are you moving back into the house. If you want to come home, you have to live in the garage." So I camped out with my waterbed, my five cats, and my father's Corvair. I remember sitting in that garage one day, on the edge of my bed, thinking, "I have lost my mind. What in the world am I doing in this condition?" I knew that my life was in ruins and that I had no one to blame but me. I felt shattered, broken, and worthless. With no job and no direction, my life was a mess. I wondered if anything good would ever become of me.

But God had a plan for me! This plan began to reveal itself through my mother, who had recently become a Christian. Guess what she was doing. She had been praying for me. Week after week, my mom had faithfully written my name on a piece of paper and taken it with her to her prayer meetings. Everyone there would lay hands on the piece of paper and pray for me to be delivered from my messed-up life. She would pray and pray and pray. I remember saying to her one day, "Mom, would you please stop praying? My life is already a mess. You're making it worse!" I just knew my problems had something to do with all the praying she did. Well, what I said to her is exactly what a Christian wants to hear, so she prayed even more!

During this time, there seemed to be "Jesus freaks" everywhere in California — on the street corner at Hollywood and Vine in Los Angeles, down at Laguna Canyon in Orange County, and in the Haight-Ashbury district of San Francisco. They were sharing the love of Jesus whether you wanted to hear it or not. You couldn't get away from them. I vividly remember a guy named Arthur Blessed who walked down a major street, dragging a life-size wooden cross and telling us to "Repent, for the Kingdom of God is at hand!" Yet these "Jesus freaks" were so sincere and caring. They invited strangers into their coffeehouses for free coffee or, if you were hungry, a warm bowl of soup. The only catch was that you had to listen to their message. This message was about love — real love — God's love. I decided to visit one of these coffeehouses. They offered me a free copy of the Gospel of John and told me that it contained what I was searching for. They also distributed a newspaper called the *Hollywood Free Paper* to anyone who would take one. I took one. This paper had information about the Jesus Movement. It also listed places where you could go if you needed help. The Jesus Movement was aggressively reaching out to my lost generation.

Druggies, red freaks, speed freaks, prostitutes, heroin addicts, and alcoholics by the droves were finding Jesus and getting on fire for Him.

On another day, back in my parents' garage in Covina, California, once again sitting on my waterbed, I slowly realized that I was wasting my life with drugs. I thought about the things my mom had been telling me about Jesus. I also thought about what the "Jesus freaks" had said about His love for me. I remember thinking, "Jesus, if You're real, if You're really, really real, then show me."

Immediately, I got up and went into the house looking for my mom. I asked her, "Where is that Calvary Chapel you've been talking about? You know, the place where kids go in their bib overalls and bare feet and the guys have long hair and beards? Where it's just like back in the days of Jesus and some guy with a bald head talks about God?" She said, "You know what? You stay right here and I'll find out for you." She started making phone calls to all her friends, and because it was only Wednesday, they kept telling her, "Can't she wait until Saturday? They have a big concert there every Saturday night, and we take several vanloads of kids to it. She can go with us." But my mom said, "No, no, I have to get those directions now." She later told me that she specifically had heard the Lord say to her, "Today is the day of salvation." She just knew she had to get me to Costa Mesa. She brought out a recent copy of the *Hollywood Free Paper* that one of the Jesus Freaks had given me. There were a lot of Christian communes listed on the back. If you needed help, all you had to do was call one of these communes, and the house elders would assist you. So my mom gave me directions to Calvary Chapel Costa Mesa, saying, "When you get down to that area, just call one of these numbers, and they'll help you."

I called a friend, and together we went down to Costa Mesa. We ended up at the Berean House, one of Calvary Chapel's communal living houses. The residents would bring in kids off the streets and share the gospel with them. Then the kids would be saved, baptized in the Holy Spirit, and baptized with water. My friend and I were really drawn to that place.

The brothers and sisters were so accommodating and loving. There was something different going on there, something special. I remember one particular hippie guy sitting cross-legged on the floor in front of a coffee table reading through a huge Bible page by page. His cheeks glowed so much that I thought he was an angel and I sensed that we were on holy ground. They invited us to stay for dinner and Bible study. I'll never forget what happened—it's so clear in my mind that it seems like it was just yesterday. The Bible study that night was about Jesus leaving the 99 sheep and searching for the one that was lost. The way the teacher described that lost sheep, I thought to myself, "He's talking to me! All these kids are packed into this room, and he's talking just to *me!*" It made such an impression upon my heart. Nobody else needed to be there. I knew that Jesus was reaching out and showing Himself to me.

When we left the Berean House that night, my friend and I decided to go down to the beach before heading back home. We sat on the sand gazing at the water. I remember watching the waves crash on the shore and thinking about everything that had happened that day. My friend lit a joint and started to "drop" acid. That is the term we used for LSD. He handed the joint to me, but I didn't take it. Instead, I said to him, "Not right now." He scornfully replied, "Oh, come on, Gail. You're not going to fall for all that Jesus stuff, are you?" I replied, "I don't know, but if I take a hit I will come down from what I am experiencing. I don't understand it, I don't know what is going on, but something wonderful is taking place deep within my heart."

While sitting on the sand looking out at the vast ocean, I realized that I had finally found what I had been desperately looking for. I gave my heart to Jesus that night.

Within a week later, I moved into the Berean House. I spent the next eight years living in various Christian communal houses. We practiced living like the early church in the book of Acts. The residents shared everything and truly were brothers and sisters—a spiritual family. There was no immorality. God had renewed His morals in our hearts, making us pure again. For many of us, these were the very same morals we had been taught while we were growing up. We had a renewed vision and Christian standards by which to live. It was truly wonderful.

I never went back to my old life. I never took another drug. Jesus died for me—He died for my pain, my tears, my guilt, and my shame. He forgave me and washed me white as snow. I was a brand-new person. I didn't understand it all, but I knew I had been given a fresh start. At my worst, when I no longer had a reason to live, when I thought I couldn't continue, Jesus was there. He took me as His own. No matter where I had been, no matter what I had done, He claimed me as a jewel in His crown. Who can refuse such love? I fell right into the arms of Jesus, which had always been open and waiting for me.

So there I was—a happy camper! I was a content sister in the Lord, baptized in the Holy Ghost, sold out to Jesus, serving Him, excited about everything, and enjoying my new family in the Lord. By this time, the Jesus Movement was making front-page headlines. Revival had erupted in a generation that the world deemed "lost." People said that we had lost not only our minds, but also our way. They said that nothing good would ever come of us and that we were just "druggies" and nothing more. But revival came with much power and might. We were delivered from what we thought was Utopia, what we thought was love. The world called us Jesus People, and we loved that title. We flooded into a crowded tent at Calvary Chapel in Costa Mesa to hear the Word of God night after night after night.

I was very happy and completely settled down. Just when I thought things couldn't get any better, I was soon to experience a wonderful change. A few friends and I decided to go see a certain "Brother Steve" way out in the desert city of Victorville, California. Steve had been one of the elders in a Christian communal house in Santa Ana. He had felt called by God to move to Victorville. He thought he was going to be like the apostle Paul, establishing all kinds of Christian communes throughout the world. The irony is that Brother Steve was just about as stubborn, strong-willed, and stiff-headed as the apostle Paul! He had no plans to ever get married. His ambition was to save the world!

Throughout that day, unknown to me at the time, the Lord had been speaking to Steve, telling him that I was supposed to be his wife! He questioned his thoughts, reasoning, "I'm going to be like the apostle Paul; I'm going to evangelize the world. This can't be God telling me I should get married." He even rebuked Satan for bringing these thoughts to his mind. But even after my friends and I left his desert commune, he was not able to stop thinking about me. A week later, out of desperation, he called me because he felt God said, "You are really going to miss out on something here." "Okay," he thought, "I'll call her and ask her to come back to see me." He did not expect me to respond the way I did. However, God had also been preparing my heart. For some time, I had been feeling like I was at a standstill in life. Though I was content, I was still waiting on God, wanting Him to do something miraculous. Even though I was only three months old in the Lord, I knew that there was a call of God on my life. When Brother Steve called to invite me back to Victorville, I didn't hesitate to tell him I was on my way. I knew that God wanted me to go. Steve on the other hand, hung up the telephone and said to himself, "Oh, no, she's coming! Now what do I do?"

On the way to Victorville, the Lord spoke so clearly to me it seemed almost audible. He told me that I would not be going back to Costa Mesa. He said that what I had been praying about, what I had been seeking, was to be presented to me in Victorville. I was very excited. I thought that perhaps I would be the elder sister in this new commune. I wasn't sure what was going to happen, but I knew it was going to be good. We were both caught up in a revival, so when God said, "Go!" we went, and when God said, "Wait!" we waited. Whenever He said to do something, we just did it! That evening Steve Mays proposed to me and I accepted. Then he asked me if I had a boyfriend. When I told him that I didn't, he said with excitement, "Great, then there is no reason to wait!" A week and a half later, on January 16, 1972, we were married. Remember that we were in the midst of a revival! I just knew it was the right thing to do. God's hand was upon us, and now, some 34 years later, we are still going strong and are more in love than ever!

Our son, Nathan, was born a year later on January 7, 1973. He is a marvelous man, and God is doing a great work in Nathan's heart. Heather, our little daughter, came along a year and a half later on September 25, 1974. When the nurse laid that baby girl into my arms, I was so blessed. For me, it felt like the Lord was pouring out His goodness, mercy, and faithfulness on me. I had been given another chance. In my mind, I had done such a terrible thing by giving away one little girl. Would God trust me with another? When Heather was born, it was as if God said to me, "Your sins I remember no more; you are truly forgiven."

I was a blessed woman with a loving husband, two beautiful children, and a thriving ministry. Life couldn't have been better. However, in the back of my mind, I always wondered about the baby girl I had given up for adoption. What had happened to her? Back then, I had agreed to what is called a "closed" adoption, in which the birth mother relinquishes all rights to her child. According to those terms, I could never know anything about her, not even where she was. However, that arrangement failed to discourage me. So with a bit of my old hippie mentality, I knew there had to be a way to beat the system. From that point on I was determined to one day find my baby!

Ever since I had given my life to Jesus, God had consistently made the impossible possible. With the Lord's leading, I decided the time had come for me to look for my baby. She was 14 years old by then. My search began in January 1984 with the help of my good friend Karyn Johnson. By the grace of God, I found my daughter after only six months. However, it took two years for me to find the courage to make any contact. Instead, I waited upon the Lord for the right timing. When I finally met my daughter Julie, I was blessed to discover that she'd grown up in a marvelous family. Julie told me that she had always had two desires. One was that her birth mother would someday find her. The other was that she would resemble her birth mother. Both of her desires have been granted. It's true! She does look like me quite a bit! In fact, we are similar in many ways. We have the same decorating style, we both like the same colors, and we are both fond of cats!

The day we met was extremely nerve-wracking and very frightening for all of us. Still, it was exciting, marvelous, and timely. I wanted to do something for her, so I decided to present her with a little gift. During that time, I had a hobby of making replicas of the soft-sculpted Cabbage Patch dolls that were popular at the time. I also sewed clothes for them. I had taken a special interest in these dolls because of their "adoption" motif, which was part of the manufacturer's marketing technique. My gift to Julie was a doll that I had made especially for the occasion. I was pleased to discover that she loved dolls, bunnies, and bears, just like I did. The Lord immediately fused our hearts together. A very special friendship was born between us. It has been a most marvelous thing! Her mother told me that after I had left, Julie sat holding the doll and said, "See, Mom, she never forgot me."

Mothers face many challenges with their children. The greatest is probably completely and wholeheartedly entrusting their children to the Lord. God created mothers to be nurturing. He intended for them to be protective of their children. However, He also requires that mothers ultimately surrender their children to His care. When I trusted the Lord to reunite me with my first daughter in His perfect timing, He blessed our reunion beyond my wildest expectations. A short time after my reunion with Julie, I was challenged again to entrust my second daughter, Heather, to God's care. There comes a time in every mother's life when she has done everything she can possibly do for her children. Then she must entrust her children to God.

When Heather was 17, she ran away from home. Talk about feeling like a failure! I was devastated. The pain of not knowing if she was safe was paralyzing. I had no idea where she was or even if I would ever see her again. In a fit of hysteria, I cried out to God, "What is going on, Lord? What have I done wrong? What's happening here?" Suddenly, the phone rang. It was Kay Smith, who had just heard that Heather had run away. I remember thinking, "Lord, You sure do answer prayer quickly." She told me something that I have never forgotten. "Gail," she said, "I have a word for you. God is at work, and this situation that you are going through is necessary so that God can make you the woman He has called you to be." She gave me a verse out of 1 Peter and told me to never, ever forget it because it would carry me through all my trials for the rest of my life. She went on to quote the passage, "*Wherein ye greatly rejoice, though now for a season . . .*" She assured me that it wouldn't be forever and "*if need be* (or because it is necessary) *ye are in heaviness through manifold temptations: that the trial of your faith, being much more precious than of gold that perisheth, though it be tried with fire, might be found unto praise and honor and glory at the appearing of Jesus Christ*" (1 Peter 1:6-7). Kay was telling me to trust the Lord with my daughter. He was using this trial to strengthen my faith. Oh, how I needed that word at that very moment to help me through my crisis!

Although it seemed like an eternity, Heather surfaced three weeks later, just a few days before her 18th birthday, only to permanently move out. I remember standing in her empty room shortly after she had left. Everything she owned was gone. It was such a horrible feeling of emptiness. All I could think was, "Nobody told me I would miss her like this." I went to my room to curl up in my special chair—a place my whole family knows is where I go to meet God. Sitting in my chair was Heather's very special Cabbage Patch doll. His name is Bartholomew—Barth for short. Immediately my mind flashed back to the day we had first "adopted" him. We had waited for weeks, not knowing if we would get a boy doll or a girl doll. We had been so excited about getting a Cabbage Patch doll. Heather insisted that Barth keep his original name. There were so many wonderful memories associated with that doll. We took him everywhere—to church, to restaurants, to the grocery store, to the mall, to the park, and even on vacations. All of those memories came flooding back to me the moment I saw Barth on my special chair. I picked him up and held him tightly, sobbing.

Then something miraculous happened. At that moment it was as if Heather was standing in front of me, saying, "Mommy, don't give up on me." There I sat in my chair, holding her doll, crying out to the Lord, "Please, Lord, what is going on?" Then God spoke to my heart: "I want my gift back." I asked, "What gift?" He answered me gently, "Children are a gift from the Lord, and I want My gift back." I said, "This isn't easy, Lord!" He ministered to my heart that day and said, "Good and faithful servant, you have done what I've asked; now you are going to have to trust Me with her. Let her go." I answered, "With Your help, I'll let her go." It was the hardest thing that God had ever asked me to do.

Heather eventually returned home. She had been back for about six months when she married a young man named Anthony. Then, in the winter of 1995, Heather and Anthony gave us a beautiful grandson.

Not even a year later, our family once again faced a huge mountain of faith. In November 1996, when our grandson was only 10 months old, we buried his father. Our son-in-law was killed in a gang-related incident at the age of 23. We were all devastated. Once more, I was challenged to trust that the Lord would allow something good to come from this terrible experience. Even in the midst of this difficult time, we found hope in His presence and His promises.

In Hebrews 12:1-2, we are encouraged to *"run with endurance the race that is set before us, looking unto Jesus, the author and finisher of our faith."*

Jesus is not just the author of our faith; He is its finisher also. Because of this truth, we can trust Him with the most devastating and confusing of circumstances, knowing that He will ultimately work in the midst of them for our good and His glory.

My daughter's husband certainly did not expect to die at such a young age. In reality, none of us knows when our life will end and we will have to stand before God. If God decided that it was your time to meet Him, right now, would you be ready? Would you have asked Jesus to come into your heart and forgive your sins? Would He say to you, "Enter into the joy of the Lord"? If not, all you have to do is simply pray, "Jesus, forgive me of all my sins. I open the door of my heart and invite You to come in and be Lord of my life."

God has taught me the importance of unconditional love through a lifetime of experiences. Unconditional love, God's love, has no strings attached and expects nothing in return. All I have to do is allow God's love to flow through me and on to others.

I have set up housekeeping with Romans 8:28, which is my life Scripture verse. Every time I read it, every time I apply it to a circumstance or a tragedy that I am going through, I gain new depth in it. It tells me—and I paraphrase—that all things work together for good for those who love God, those who will cooperate with Him knowing that He is using these things to conform us into the image of Christ. What have I learned through the years? God has taught me to see His hand in everything that comes my way. In addition, I have learned to believe in the power of prayer. This is very important because, well, it works. I have a little motto: *Turn your cares into prayers!*

There is only one thing I would change about my life. If I could, I would give my life to Jesus much, much sooner than I did. Thirty-four years ago, I was just a lost, wayward, confused kid looking for answers to life. Today, I am serving the Lord with the same fervency that I felt when I first found Jesus. I am blessed to have been a part of the Jesus Movement, the great revival that transformed a lost generation into Jesus People. My dear husband feels the same way. He has devoted his life to the call of God and has the same passion for Jesus now that he did when he was first saved. I am abundantly blessed as a mother, as a grandmother, as a pastor's wife, and as the leader of a ministry that is teaching women to be godly in a very ungodly world.

Biography

Gail is the wife of Pastor Steve Mays, who has served at Calvary Chapel South Bay, located in the Los Angeles, California area for 25 years. Gail and Steve have been a vital part of the Calvary Chapel movement for 35 years. Although she is involved in a variety of activities, the one thing she loves to do most is to minister to women. She takes every opportunity to instruct them in the Word of God, believing that it alone has the power to change a life!

Jean McClure

Every Mother's Dream

*"Behold, I have set before thee an open door, and no man
can shut it: for thou hast a little strength, and hast kept my
word, and hast not denied my name."*
Revelation 3:8, KJV

Have you ever kept a book of remembrance? By that I mean have
you written down the things that God has done for you—the trials and
the victories, the answers to prayer, the promises from His Word for your
prodigal, for your marriage, for illness or finances? In the Old Testament
the Lord told the children of Israel to keep a book of remembrance of
all that God had done for them so that they could tell their children and
their children's children.

My mom had Alzheimer's Disease, and when she passed away at age eighty-five, my dad eventually moved and gave me an old, white, French-provincial bedroom set that had been mine when I was a little girl. Stuck between the drawers, I found a little spiral notebook. I opened it up and discovered that in it my mom had written the story of her life. She had written it when she was in the early stages of Alzheimer's. She knew that she was losing her memory and wanted to pass on the stories she wouldn't be able to tell us. Her book of remembrance was truly a treasure. We had copies made and gave them to all the grandchildren at my dad's ninetieth birthday party. What a testimony it was to read about how God had led in their life together. How fascinating it is to look back on one's life and see that truly the Lord has been leading all along the way.

One of my earliest memories is of my mother teaching child evangelism classes when I was in grade school. We went into homes and she told Bible stories using flannel-graph lessons. There were prizes for the children who had memorized Scripture and for those who had brought friends. I liked to paint with watercolors and I often helped her with crafts, so one day she asked me to decorate a sheet of paper with the lyrics to the hymn, "Great is Thy Faithfulness" written on it. While I was painting the song sheet, I learned this ancient hymn:

> *"Great is Thy faithfulness, O God my Father;*
> *There is no shadow of turning with Thee;*
> *Thou changest not, Thy compassions, they fail not . . .*
> *All I have needed Thy hand hath provided;*
> *Great is Thy Faithfulness, Lord, unto me!"* [8]

Through the years I have realized that its lyrics have been true in my life, and on the day I opened that notebook, I found that they had been true in my parents' lives as well.

My mother, Marguerite, grew up in Minneapolis, Minnesota, in the early 1900s. She was the youngest of twelve children. She and her sister,

Frieda, were very close. When Aunt Frieda was eighteen years old and my mom was twelve years old, Aunt Frieda went to a tent meeting in downtown Minneapolis. In those days, evangelists and preachers would go from city to city and put up big circus tents, sometimes with sawdust on the floors to keep the dust down. People's lives were much simpler then, so when an evangelist came to town, it would be a big event—like a mini-Harvest Crusade—and people would be drawn in. The gospel would be preached and people would get saved. That first night when Aunt Frieda went to the meeting, she asked the Lord Jesus into her heart, and her life was turned upside down. She came home wanting her sister to find what she had found. She said to my mother, "If you will go to the tent meeting with me tomorrow night, I'll give you a watch." My mother didn't want to go, but when Aunt Frieda offered the watch, she thought, *You know, I think I could work that tent meeting into my schedule.*

The following night, both my mother and my grandmother received Christ. Aunt Frieda did follow through with her promise and bought my mother a watch that was better than her own. It took her months to pay it off and it was a treasure in my mom's life. How wonderful to sacrifice for the salvation of others! My siblings and I always said that it was because of Aunt Frieda that we too found Christ.

My mom went to nursing school at the University of Minnesota where she met my dad, who was studying to become a doctor. Mom was late to class one day because there had been a robbery in her dormitory, and the precious watch that Aunt Frieda had given her had been stolen. She was so brokenhearted that she didn't care if she missed class. The dorm mother caught her and her roommate and ordered them to get going. They obeyed, but when they got there, they discovered that they had been locked out. (There was no sympathy for being late in those days; the teacher would simply lock the door.) They sat on the front steps of the university feeling sorry for themselves. Three interns noticed these two cute nursing students looking forlorn on the front steps, so they went outside to meet them. That's how my parents met. They were married seven years later, after Dad had finished medical school. People were very practical in those days and long engagements were common.

My dad, Philip, was not a Christian when Mom married him. She didn't know that the Scripture says, "Do not be unequally yoked" (see 2 Corinthians 6:14), which means Christians are not to marry non-Christians. But after she married him, she knew there was a problem. Some members of his family were very critical of her because of her faith. They thought she would ruin my dad and that he wouldn't be fun to be around anymore. Nevertheless, she was firm in her faith and began to pray diligently for his salvation.

Every day she and a neighbor got together to pray for him—even in the dead of winter, with a foot of snow on the ground. She loved him so much, and she wanted him to find what she had found. She would drag him to church, and because he loved her, he would go. One Sunday while they were sitting in church, the pastor introduced his sermon with the title, "Oh, Philip, have you been so long with Me and have not known Me?" (see John 14:9). In this passage, Jesus was speaking to one of His disciples. But my dad about fell off the pew. He said to my mom, "You told that minister about me, didn't you?" She insisted, "No I didn't. I didn't say anything."

God began to pursue my dad like the hound of heaven. He would be shaving and Scriptures like, *Though your sins are like scarlet, they shall be as white as snow* (Isaiah 1:18), would come into his mind and he would quote them out loud and say, "What is that all about?" The problem was that my dad was a medical doctor and everything had to be proven in a test tube for him to believe it. There was no room for faith in the world of science. On his first day of medical school, the professor had gotten up and said scornfully, *None of you here believes in God, do you?* He instilled doubt in the minds of students who would have highly respected him. And so, through the years, my dad struggled with believing in something he couldn't see. But he knew there had to something out there bigger than himself. Creation is too perfect.

Approximately five years after my parents were married, he became very ill with pneumonia. He had a fever of 105 degrees and he knew he was in big trouble. My mother sent the minister to talk to him about Jesus every day while he was in the hospital. After a while the minister became so frustrated because my dad questioned everything. The idea that one's sins could be forgiven by faith in Jesus was too illogical for him. Finally the preacher said, "Phil, don't you want to be saved?" He had grown tired of trying to convince my dad and didn't want to visit him anymore. My dad later said that at that point *he knew that he knew* that it was his last opportunity to come to Christ. The Scripture tells us, *My Spirit shall not always strive with a man* (Genesis 6:3). He prayed, "All right, Lord Jesus, in blind faith, I reach out and accept You as my Lord and Savior." In an instant, all those Scriptures that he had not understood became clear to him. He said it felt like a light bulb went on in his head. He got well, went home from the hospital, and his whole life changed.

It was into this Christian home that I was born. My father was studying at the Mayo Clinic in Rochester, Minnesota. He had been a general practitioner for thirteen years, and during his last month in general practice, he had delivered twenty-five babies. That is almost a baby a day. He was exhausted, performing surgery all morning, seeing patients all afternoon, and delivering babies all night. So at the age of forty, he went back to school to specialize. My mother was forty-two years old and my dad was forty-three years old when I was born. (They already had two sons and I think I was a surprise.) When I was one-year-old, we moved to Pasadena, California, and my dad set up a new practice.

My parents were saved. But being born into a Christian family doesn't automatically make one a Christian. There's a saying: God does not have grandchildren, He only has children. Some people will say, "I'm a Christian," and if they are asked what makes that so, they will say, "Well, I'm

American. I eat apple pie, I go to baseball games, and I believe in God." None of these things make someone a Christian. Everyone has to say yes to Jesus for themselves.

One summer my folks bought a little cabin at a Christian conference center called Mount Hermon, near Santa Cruz, California. Speakers like Billy Graham and Jay Vernon McGee would come to speak. One June night when I was seven years old, I was sitting in the second row during an evening service at the conference center and the speaker asked if anyone wanted to receive Jesus. I don't remember what else he said, but the conviction of the Holy Spirit was heavy upon me, and I raised my hand to accept the Lord. My mother looked at me and said, "Honey, you've already received the Lord," but I didn't remember doing so before that night and tears began to run down my face. The man next to me said, "Honey, don't let anyone stop you from accepting Jesus." He must have thought my mom was a bad person. She wasn't. She kept quiet the minute she saw me crying. This is the time I would pinpoint as having really understood the gospel and having received Christ. I was on my way to heaven, and that was really wonderful. I began to be still before the Lord that summer, and my mom would kneel by my bed at night and pray with me. My walk with God began to grow ever so slowly.

One night a couple of summers later, when I was about to enter junior high school, I had a dream. I rarely remember my dreams, but this one was so vivid—I clearly remembered every detail when I woke up. I dreamt that I had cancer in one of my legs and had six months to live. I remember thinking, *If I only have six months to live, what am I going to do with those six months? I've got to tell people about Jesus.* (A sure sign that you are born again is when you want to share the gospel.) In my dream, I went to a shopping area near my home where shoppers were rushing here and there with their purchases. I stood in the midst of this crowd and said, "Stop! Stop! There's a road right here, and it's very narrow, but it goes to heaven. You are going down the broad road. You've got to turn around and go down the narrow road. It will lead you to Christ, and He will take you on to heaven." Most people walked past as if they hadn't heard me. But every once in a while, someone would stop and listen to me, and they would turn and go down the narrow road. When I woke up in the morning, I heard the Lord clearly say to me, "In that dream you knew exactly how long you had to live. Today you don't. So no matter how long you have to live, know what is most important—and that is Me. Share Me with others." So even at a young age the Lord impressed upon me the reason I am alive.

First John 5:12 says, *He who has the Son has life; he who does not have the Son of God does not have life.* I was saved and I had life. But God wasn't through with me yet. There was this little area called surrender. Don't you hate that word? One day my dad called me into the den. He was sitting in his big, old, red, leather chair, and he said, "I want to teach you a verse." The verse was 1 John 2:15. It says, *Love not the world, neither the things that are in the world. If any man loves the world, the love of the Father is not in him* (KJV). Now that might seem like a strange verse to teach a child, but it was very good for me. I thought, *Well, isn't that a great verse? That's nice. "Love not the world." Okay.* But then, as I grew up I realized that my father was trying to teach me that the things that are important are the things of God. As it says in 1 John 2:17, *The world passeth away, and the lust thereof: but he that doeth the will of God abideth forever* (KJV).

In their desire to train me up in the ways of the Lord, my folks decided to do something very unusual when I finished junior high school. They

> First John 5:12 says, *He who has the Son has life; he who does not have the Son of God does not have life. I was saved and I had life. But God wasn't through with me yet. There was this little area called surrender.*

decided that I needed to go to a Christian boarding school. It was much cheaper in those days than it is today and I wouldn't recommend this to everybody because I think God has an individual plan for each family and for each child. But my parents' plan was to send me three thousand miles away from home to Hampden du Bose Academy near Orlando, Florida. A group of us took a three-day train ride to Chicago, and then down through the South. I entered boarding school as a fourteen-year-old, and I went there all four years of high school.

I learned a great deal from the experience. Billy Graham's daughters were my roommates, the Billy Graham team kids went there, as did missionary kids from all over the world. One of my very best friends was a girl named Marilyn Spees, whose parents were missionaries to the Pigmies (the Baca tribe) in Africa. She taught me what it is to live by faith. Another good friend was the daughter of Nate Saint, who was martyred in Ecuador along with Jim Elliot and three others.

There were a couple hundred students in the school, but one girl in particular changed my life. I really admired her walk with the Lord. Her name was Lolly Sutton. We were roommates and we were both from Southern California, so we bonded. She was a junior and I was a lowly freshman. One day we were running on the track for Phys Ed and Lolly said, "Jean, have you ever thought about going into full-time Christian work?" The Lord had called her to be a missionary to South America when she was a freshman. She asked, "Would you be interested in serving the Lord for the rest of your life?" I thought, *I am young and I have my whole life ahead of me.* So I answered, "Lolly, I have a brother who has talked about being a missionary to Africa. And I think one per family is a pretty good quota. Besides, I'm not really big into eating monkey heads and living in huts, and I don't care for bugs. Lolly, I don't think so." It didn't sound like fun to me. She didn't say anything else.

One year later I was a lowly sophomore and she was a big senior. We were sitting in church together one day and the speaker didn't say anything memorable, but I was challenged when he asked the question, *Is there anyone who wants to commit their life to full-time Christian service?* The Holy Spirit prompted me to put my hand up and say yes. In my heart I was struggling terribly. I didn't want to do it. But I was compelled, *Put your hand up. This is an important decision for your life.* It was at that moment that I knew someone was fervently praying. As soon as the service was over, I turned to Lolly and asked, "Have you been praying that I would go to the mission field or go into full-time Christian work?" She said "Oh, what ever made you think of that?" I demanded that she tell me the truth. Finally, she admitted that she had been praying for me ever since our conversation the previous year. This upper-classman had bothered to spend twelve months praying for an under-classman. Wow!

Lolly later married and went to the mission field just as she had planned. One day I got a phone call telling me that she had died suddenly from a brain tumor. She was in her early thirties. I can't wait to get to heaven and tell Lolly how grateful I am that she spent twelve months praying for me and how it changed my life forever. I'm reminded of my Aunt Frieda, and I often have to ask myself the question: *Do I sacrifice for others the way these young women did?*

I went back to my room that night and waited until all my roommates were asleep. I knelt down on the floor beside my bunk and I had it out with the Lord. You see, I was saved. I knew I was going to heaven. I had a walk with the Lord. But I didn't quite want to give Him everything because that meant He could be the boss of me. And I struggle with Him or anyone else being my boss. I said, "Lord, let's talk about this. Lolly's been praying for me, and if I tell You that I will give up my life to follow You anywhere You want me to go, I know You're going to send me to India. I just know it! I really like hamburgers, and they don't eat cows there. I don't like bugs, and they have a lot of them in India. And You know what, Lord? If I go to India, my family and friends are going to forget me. No one will ever marry me because no one will want to go to India with me. That's all right; I can be single. But if You want me to get married, how will that happen in India?" Finally I said, "Lord, India does not accept American citizens as missionaries." (In those days it was rare for an American citizen to serve as a missionary in India. British citizens were normally the only missionaries allowed into the country.)

I presented my best argument and then I was quiet. I heard Him clearly speak to my heart. He said, "Tell me what you brought with you when you were born." And I thought, *Hmm. I didn't bring a purse. So I didn't have any money. I didn't bring any friends. I didn't even bring clothes. I didn't bring anything! I came into this world naked.* And He said, "That's exactly how you are going out. It is only your relationship with Me that you will take with you. So, now, what would you like to do with the rest of your life?" He always knows how to get me! At fifteen years of age, I knew that if I said yes to Him, I would be happy. I didn't think life would be easy, and it hasn't been. But I knew I would have joy and peace. And I knew that if I didn't surrender to Him, I was going to have a miserable life. After an intense struggle, I finally said, "Yes, Lord. I'll go wherever You want me to go." Suddenly peace flooded my heart. That's how it is when you accept the Lord or surrender to Him. You wonder, *Why did it take me so long to come to this place? It would have been so much easier if I hadn't struggled.*

In my senior year, I wrote a letter of inquiry to Dohnavur Fellowship, Amy Carmichaels's orphanage in India, asking what would be required for me to become one of their missionaries. I had read Amy Carmichael's books and had been deeply touched by her life. A staff member wrote back and told me I would need to become a physical therapist.

We had to pick a verse at graduation as our life verse, and the verse that the Lord gave me was Revelation 3:8, *Behold, I have set before thee an open door, and no man can shut it: for thou hast a little strength, and hast kept my word, and hast not denied my name* (KJV). As I sought direction as to what God's will was for my life, I knew He would lead me by opening and shutting doors before me. I felt that I had to be willing to try the door. Additionally, those things that I had once been afraid of no longer frightened me.

My mother and I went to Santa Barbara to look into a nursing school. When we got there, the school was no longer there. It had been closed down and the doors were locked. It was a clear picture that God was leading me in a different direction. I think in life God sometimes leads us to that point of completely surrendering our wills to His. And once we do, our worst fears are conquered. He makes us knock on doors, but He may not make us go through them. What matters is being willing to go wherever He leads.

Another question I asked was: "Lord, do You want me to stay single for the rest of my life?" I had a music teacher in grade school who said, "You can pray for your husband right now." I protested, "That's ridiculous. I'm in grade school." She said, "No. It's okay, because he's probably alive in the world someplace today. Don't you want to pray for him?" Through the years, I would secretly pray, "Lord, if You have a husband out there for me, be preparing him for me, as You are preparing me for him."

I met my husband at church. He was a brand-new Christian. I knew his sister-in-law, and one day she had said, "The black sheep of the McClure family has just come to the Lord, and it's so exciting. We're all so happy." He had gotten saved at a Billy Graham meeting and then had gotten involved in a men's prayer meeting that turned his life upside down. Instead of becoming a businessman as he had planned, he had been called into ministry. He was on fire for the Lord by the time I met him, and we were heading in the same direction. We fell madly in love with each other.

Don and I were married at Christmastime in 1968, graduated from college in the spring of 1969, and went to Bible college that September. A pastor named Alan Redpath had come to preach at a local church. Don loved his preaching and would follow him around to different churches to hear him. One evening we went out to dinner with Dr. Redpath and he advised Don to attend a Bible school in England called Capernwray. Don knew nothing and Dr. Redpath said, "If you want to serve the Lord, seminary is great, but first you need a better grasp of the Word of God." So we sold most of our possessions and went. God changed my husband's life incredibly and He ministered to me during our time there.

We came back from England and Don went to seminary. After a while we got involved in this little church called Calvary Chapel that his sister had invited us to. The people were bizarre. They called themselves hippies and I had never been exposed to hippies before. My dad said you could tell when they were saved because the born-again hippies had taken baths. These people were coming off drugs and they were living in Christian communes. We began to see miracles of people being healed, restored, saved, and filled with the Spirit. Pastor Chuck Smith asked my husband to come on staff, and we had the awesome privilege of being a part of a great revival called the Jesus Movement.

During this time, Dr. Redpath came for a visit, and we were afraid to take him to Calvary Chapel because of the hippies. I thought, *Oh, his hair is going to stand on end. He's going to say "You shouldn't be in this church."* The church was meeting in a huge tent while an auditorium was being built. We took him there for a Saturday night concert and couldn't drag him out of the place! He said, "This is what I've always longed to see—a move of the Holy Spirit among young people." The hippies were dressed in their raggedy clothes and had long hair. They were singing loudly, but everyone's hands were stretched to heaven in worship. It was an incredible revival and I felt privileged to be a part of it.

Chuck later sent us to a place called Lake Arrowhead, California, where Don started Calvary Chapel of Lake Arrowhead. Then he called Pastor Chuck and said, "Chuck, I've always wanted to start a Bible college like Capernwray." That was the beginning of the Calvary Chapel Bible College, which is now located in Murrieta, California.

I'm married to a guy who is like the apostle Paul; God moves him to help churches. He loves to get them started, and then we move on. After Lake Arrowhead, he pastored Calvary Chapel of Redlands, California, for eleven years. When that got going really well, Don went to Pastor Chuck and said, "Send me someplace no one else wants to go." Chuck got a big smile on his face and said, "Have I got a place for you!" It was a denominational church in San Jose, California, that had numerous problems. It appeared to be an impossible situation, but with God nothing is impossible! We stayed eleven years, and once again I found that all I had needed, God provided. In 2002 Pastor Chuck called us to return to Southern California, where we continue to serve and see the faithfulness of God in every situation.

The Lord has given us three precious sons, and they in turn have blessed us with six wonderful grandchildren. The best part, however, is that they all know Jesus. Even my parents who are in heaven now will one day meet their great-grandchildren. It is our joy to pray for our children and our children's children that they will know and follow hard after the Lord. If your parents didn't know Christ and didn't pray for you, you can be the one to do this for your loved ones.

I don't think I ever really comprehended the depth of Jesus's love for me until I had children of my own. Not because my boys loved me, although they do, but because I love them. I'm crazy about them. I obsess over them. I have unconditional love for them. I want them to have all God has for them—I want them to have happiness, joy, holiness, and fellowship with me. No matter what they did when they were little, I loved them and forgave them. Even though I had to deal with their naughtiness, I would sacrifice for them, pray for them, and wrap my arms around them and hold them. It was in those times that I understood that Jesus did the same thing for me because He loved me. This is what an earthly parent does and this is what our heavenly Father does as well.

If an earthly parent loves his or her children so very much, how much more must our heavenly Father love us? I am certainly a sinner, and yet, He loves me. The depth of His love is unfathomable.

I remember sitting in a home Bible study that my husband was teaching in Costa Mesa in the middle of the Jesus Movement. Don explained the baptism of the Holy Spirit and asked if anyone wanted to receive it. The understanding of this whole concept began to come alive for me and I longed for Jesus to fill me and to immerse me in His Spirit. I raised my hand that night. The depth of my unworthiness overwhelmend me, but Jesus began to pour out His love to me—and it was in that moment that I fell in love with Him.

Great is His faithfulness! Isaiah 54:10 says, *"Though the mountains be shaken and the hills be removed, yet my unfailing love for you will not be shaken nor my covenant of peace be removed," says the LORD, who has compassion on you* (NIV). Who could resist such a faithful, loving God? He has never once failed to lead me, comfort me, strengthen me, and fill me with His peace. Never once. Though I came into this world with absolutely nothing, because He found me and I am His, I will leave some day cloaked in the richness of His presence. I am blessed beyond measure.

Biography

Jean McClure has served alongside her husband, Don, in various pastoral positions throughout the Calvary Chapel movement for more than thirty years. She currently oversees the women's ministry at Calvary Laguna in Irvine, California, where Don is senior pastor, and she is a popular retreat speaker. Jean and Don have three grown sons and six grandchildren.

Sharon Faith Ries

The Well-Trodden Path

The path of the just is like the shining sun,
that shines ever brighter unto the perfect day.
Proverbs 4:18

This is the story of my life. It is the well-trodden path that was marked for me by my godly ancestors and many other saints whom I have encountered along the way. Herein I describe the foundation upon which my life was built, the sins of my youth, and the way with which I was cleansed by the blood of Jesus Christ—the One who died for my sins, gave me His divine love for my husband, and instilled in me a passion for the salvation of souls.

I was raised in a God-fearing home with parents who also had an un-ending passion for souls. They were missionaries in South America from 1942 until 1961. The first event I remember about my life happened in Colombia in April 1951, when I was three years old. I was with my mother and my sister Shirley, who is sixteen months older than me. It was a dark and rainy day. The heavens thundered with anger. Amid flashes of lightning, I found myself climbing onto a large army aircraft and across a floor that was splattered with human blood. A sergeant, bleeding from his mouth, sat in one of the seats that lined the interior walls of the aircraft. Mother explained that the demon-possessed Colonel Villamizar had kicked the sergeant in the mouth. She prayed and nestled us both close to her as we flew to safety.

My father, Edmund Allen Farrel, was born November 27, 1916, in Springview, Nebraska. His parents, William Ryan and Dortha, were ranch-ers in Wyoming. They had six children. Grandpa William was a very fine, gentle man whose family belonged to the Mormon Church. Polygamy was practiced in that church, so Grandpa William's father decided it was a false sect and pulled his family out of it. Eventually, when Grandpa William married Grandma Dortha, he was disowned for not marrying into the sect.

When Daddy was a young boy, a chubby, little Pentecostal watchmaker named Moris lived across the street. He told Daddy Bible stories and introduced him and his family to the Lord. Before long his mother and his siblings were attending meetings in the upstairs of an old building partaking in good, old-fashioned, high-spirited Pentecostal worship. Daddy did not attend, and by the time he was sixteen, he was riding the top of a boxcar to Fresno, California, where he found work in the beet fields. He had experienced enough falsehood in the church that he decided he would never become a Christian and instead, like many young men of the day, he pursued an adventurous life.

Disappointed, he went back to Nebraska where he worked for three years in an animal slaughter house and entangled himself in a life of drinking, smoking, and partying. One icy winter night, returning home from a party discouraged and drunk, a light appeared in the sky above him as he crossed the bridge that connects Sioux City, Nebraska, with South Sioux City. He knew, by the Spirit of God, that the light was Jesus saying to him, "Follow Me." He threw the bottle of liquor into the frozen river and as he heard it smash, he determined to follow Jesus.

Days later, as was the custom during altar calls, he put his cigarettes under the altar of the little church where Grandma Dortha worshiped regularly. Three years later, Daddy graduated at the top of his class from the Open Bible College in Des Moines, Iowa. He had decided to become a missionary after being in contact with a man who worked with the Toba Indians in the "green hell" of Argentina, which borders Uruguay, Paraguay, and Brazil. As a single, twenty-five-year-old man, he would leave all, deny himself, and follow Jesus in taking the gospel to the "uttermost parts of the world" (see Acts 1:8).

My mother, Rachel Naomi Kopp, was born in Auburn, Nebraska, on December 21, 1922. Her father, Le Roy M. Kopp, was saved and called by God to preach the gospel at eighteen years of age, and he became known as "the boy preacher." His family belonged to the United Brethren Church. Her mother, Bertha Eula Mills, was the daughter of ministers in the Pilgrim Holiness movement, an offshoot of the Quakers. In her youth, Grandma Eula was rebellious against God, so her father had to prevail in prayer for her until she surrendered her life to Christ. Mother's parents breathed, lived, and preached "the holy life," which could be attainable through the blood of Jesus Christ. Their families were landowners until the depression came and took all but two of their farms.

Grandma Eula dedicated her four sons and two daughters to the work of the Lord on the mission fields of the world. Grandpa and Grandma preached the gospel for twelve years, pastoring United Brethren churches in eastern and western Kansas. In January 1929, Grandpa loaded up his family into a Model A Ford sedan and drove them to Los Angeles, California, to pastor a church belonging to the flourishing, Spirit-filled movement of the International Church of the Foursquare Gospel founded by Aimee Semple McPherson. Grandpa pastored in several cities for the next thirty years and was heard on Christian radio station KGER in Los Angeles for over forty years. When we were home on furlough from South America, my sister and I had the thrill of singing in Spanish on his radio program, *Radio Revival*.

Mother dedicated her life to Jesus at the young age of seven and was filled with the Holy Spirit when she was ten years old. Seven years later, a Spirit-filled young man held his hand above her head and prophesied her life's call: "I am calling you to the land south of the Great River." That same year, she initiated the first Interdenominational Youth Rally in the greater Los Angeles area. It was during this time that my father was passing through Los Angeles on his way to South America. While visiting Calvary Temple, Grandpa Kopp's church, he met Mother, and she asked him to speak at one of these rallies. Knowing that God had brought them together, Daddy asked Mother, "Will you go to the mission field with me?"

They were married, studied Spanish in Corpus Christi, Texas, and waited for transportation to any port in South America. With World War II erupting in 1941, the ship that was scheduled to take them to Argentina was sunk in the war. With "the call of God" burning in their hearts, they waited for God to take them to the mission field. Finally a ship embarked, leaving them in Colombia, where they spent the next nine years in the high Andes Mountains.

In November 1944 my parents' firstborn, "little Rachel," died just prior to her birth after Mother rode mule-back for five days to a hospital in Bogota, the capital city of Colombia. Mother never held her baby and Daddy never saw her, but both came to understand that God had allowed this to strengthen them for the trials and persecutions that would lay ahead. By God's sovereign will, Daddy and Mother came to know the pain and sorrow common to Colombian women. Rachel was buried in the "heretic's graveyard" of the town where they had first begun their ministry. She belonged to Jesus and would forever be spared from pain and sorrow. However, the rest of us would live that we might spread the gospel to lost souls.

Two years later, my sister Shirley Evangeline was born alive and well in Bogota, Colombia. After five years on the mission field, I was born in March 1948, in Los Angeles, California, while my parents were on furlough. Because I was to be born in the breech position, my mother was told that either one or both of us would die during childbirth. Being a woman who puts her faith in God and not in man, Mother made a covenant with her Lord: "If You will let my daughter live, I will call her Faith," and so I was named Sharon Faith.

In 1942, just months after my parents arrived as young missionaries, *La Revolucón* against the liberal government in Colombia broke out. This war has continued until today but its focus has changed; the revolutionaries are now called *la guerrilla* and the cause is drug trafficking. Religious fanatics saw the early stage of the revolution as an opportunity to stop the infiltration of Protestantism in Colombia by persecuting and killing Christian pastors and missionaries. Ranchers were told that we had hooves and horns and that they should not have anything to do with us or even look our way. Our lives were in imminent danger the entire nine years that our family lived in Colombia.

Hundreds of national pastors were martyred. One was buried up to his neck and asked to renounce God. When he refused, he was shot in the head as he offered up his life as a sacrifice to the Lord. Another was cut into pieces and his body parts were handed out to the people in his congregation. A missionary friend was dragged through the streets by her long, blond hair in order to humiliate her. Our huge mission station, which sat on a hill overlooking two great rivers, was ransacked and burnt down. After many near-death experiences and narrow escapes, my mother, my sister, and I were forced onto that bloody airplane at the point of a machine gun. Daddy was imprisoned almost a year later, and after being locked up for six weeks, was handcuffed and paraded down the streets of Villavicencio, today a thriving city where Calvary Chapel has several churches, a large Christian school, and a Bible school. My parents were living examples to me and to the world around them of the heroes of faith described in Hebrews 11, who, "By faith . . . worked righteousness, obtained promises . . . quenched the violence of fire, escaped the edge of the sword, out of weakness were made strong, became valiant in battle . . . had trial of mockings . . . chains and imprisonment" (see Hebrews 11:33–37).

Because of the danger to our lives, and the persistence of their missionary call, my parents went to Jamaica to minister for a few months until the Lord allowed them to return to Colombia for several more years. In 1952 the Lord opened the doors for us to go to Chile, where I lived from the time I was four years old until I was thirteen years old. There my parents started a grammar school for the very poor children who lived a few blocks away in "shack town" and an interdenominational Bible school where young men and women were trained to "go and make disciples of all the nations" (see Matthew 28:19). The graduates were commissioned to take the gospel to all of South America, and many subsequently planted churches. I had the opportunity to visit many churches, of many denominations, in almost every country in South America.

In Chile we experienced a different type of religious persecution. We were ridiculed many times and had fewer privileges than our Catholic classmates. However, Jews were treated worse. Not having the privilege of attending English-speaking missionary schools, Shirley and I learned and lived the Spanish culture and mastered the language. We lived in a huge mission house that had previously belonged to a Devil worshiper. When we first moved in, we heard unexplainable commotion at night. After anointing the house with oil, and after a few all-night prayer meetings, the house was freed of its evil presence.

Mother came into our room every night and told us about the protection we have through the shedding of Christ's blood for our sins. She told us that Jesus had won the victory over Satan and his demons and had put them to open shame when He triumphed over them at the cross. As far back as I can remember I knew about the cross. My mother taught us that in any danger we can call on Jesus, and that through His blood there is power to save us from sin, the world, and the Devil. My sister and I crawled into bed together at night and repeated aloud, "The blood of Jesus, the blood of Jesus," and thus we would fall asleep knowing that Christ had sacrificed His life for us so that we could be safe from Satan and all his evil forces.

My mother played five instruments, wrote songs, and translated dozens of hymns, so Shirley and I grew up singing. The songs about the blood of Jesus were very special to me. As we prayed, my mother would talk about our burdens and remind us that by faith we could place them at the foot of the cross. We would sing, "At the cross, at the cross where I first saw the light, and the burden of my heart rolled away. . . ." I didn't have a lot of burdens at that young age—Mother and Daddy carried them all for me then—but I believed by faith that the blood shed on the cross of Christ would take away the burden of sin. I could rest and sleep in that truth. Never did I imagine that these songs would literally get me through some of the most difficult and trying times in my life, the "dark nights of the soul" that lay ahead for me.

I remember singing:

> "On a hill far away stood an old rugged cross,
> The emblem of suffering and shame . . .
> So I'll cherish the old rugged cross,
> Till my trophies at last I lay down;
> I will cling to the old rugged cross,
> And exchange it some day for a crown." [9]

I would sing joyfully, neither realizing what it meant to cherish the cross nor understanding why it is the "emblem of suffering and shame." But in time I came to cherish it and to understand that Jesus took my sin and the shame it has brought into my life and nailed it to the cross with Him so that I do not have to bear it anymore. Praise be to God!

After twenty-one years on the mission field, my parents felt that they needed to take their daughters to the United States so that we could get to know our families, study in English, and learn about our American culture. God was calling us to a new and different life. He had a plan for us! It was very traumatic for me at the age of thirteen to leave my lifetime friends, the Latin culture, and the beautiful country of Chile, with its diverse landscapes lined by the immense Andes Mountains.

What a joy it was to meet Mother's and Daddy's families. They demonstrated so much love and blessed us with all the things that we needed to live in America. They were a loving expression of God's tender care for His servants. We worshiped together with aunts, uncles, and cousins at Calvary Temple in Los Angeles. Grandpa Kopp and Uncles Paul Kopp and Herbie Cass kept us spellbound as they passionately shared the Word of God. In his latter years, Grandpa was called by God to go on short-term mission trips to Israel. My cousin, Charles Kopp, and his family have been serving there for over thirty-nine years.

Grandma was a tender spiritual mother to her large family and their friends. She often fasted and "prayed through" for a family member who was going through a trying time until she had an answer from God through His Word. She told us about the time that her dad sent her to her room to "pray through" when she received a thirteen-page love letter from Grandpa, who wanted to marry her. She obeyed and later recalled, "God gave me a divine love for Grandpa that has withheld the test of time." She faithfully paid her tithes and gave generous offerings to those in the family who were in ministry. She blessed us all on the holidays with her amazing baking and many spiritual blessings, which included laying hands on us in prayer and singing hymns of worship and adoration to our Lord. It was wonderful to learn that America had its beginnings with the Pilgrims who were God-fearing, humble people searching for freedom of worship. In America I found a place where I could worship my God with all my heart, mind, and soul in peace—and finally, without persecution. My dream, however, was to go back to the only life I really knew—the missionary life.

When I was in high school, our family attended the Church of God (Cleveland, Tennessee) in Baldwin Park, California. Our pastor, Carl Green, was a holy man of prayer who had a passion for the lost in our city. He spoke directly to us young people and wept at times as he challenged us to give our lives to Jesus. I responded often to his pleadings, kneeling at the altar in prayer and consecrating my life to the Lord. I loved singing in the choir and performing in church plays. My life revolved around church.

During my junior year in high school, a handsome, Spanish young man named Raul Ries began to take a special interest in me. I caught him looking at me often and he caught me looking back! However, he never asked me for a date. He later told me that it was because I was a "church girl" and the "marrying kind." I heard that he got into a lot of fights, but it seemed to me that most boys did. I longed for a godly boyfriend. However, after a bad relationship with a church boy, and against my parents' instruction, dating non-believers didn't seem so bad. Besides, I had no intention of marrying anybody until I had attended Bible college.

My passion was to serve God in South America. I had answered the call of God many times as a young girl. When we were on furlough visiting churches, after Daddy showed the missionary slide presentation, he would plead for Christians to go and take the gospel to unreached regions. "Who will go?" he would plead, and I would answer in the secret place of my heart, "I will go. Send me."

However, I could not get Raul out of my mind. Seeing him every day at school did not help. "If only he knew God," I thought, "he would be perfect for me." He was exciting, and his stride and demeanor told me that he had great goals in life. So did I.

I was very involved in school activities, and in my junior year my classmates elected me "Sport Princess." I asked Raul to escort me to the event and introduced a well-behaved young man to my missionary parents. They were loving to Raul and immediately started praying for his conversion. That night, I invited him to church. He did not ask me out again. I was so busy with school and church that I was just fine with getting a glimpse of him daily at school. I was confident that if God had chosen Raul for me, He would save him. I had seen thousands of people get saved. I simply did not worry about it.

In my senior year I was honored again by my classmates and was elected to be one of the homecoming princesses at the annual homecoming football game. Again I asked Raul to escort me, but this time he had gotten kicked out of school for fighting. "Oh, it was just a little scuffle," he explained it away. I liked the fact that he was strong and feisty. He was going into the United States Marine Corps when we graduated. He was a man of war. He was fascinating to me.

In 1966 the Vietnam War was in full swing and many of our classmates were sent into combat. Some had already been wounded; some had even died. Raul would probably also be sent to war. To my surprise, he asked me to spend our senior party together before he went to boot camp. I was crazy about him. I had waited two years for him to ask me out. I was desperate to be with him and I was no longer thinking much about how God viewed our relationship. That night Raul kissed me. I knew then that I would be with him forever. We were on a ship on the way to Catalina Island, off the coast of Southern California. The sky was brilliant with the light of the moon and a billion stars. A straying, bright shooting-star intercepted my life and was leading me on an unknown path. I took my eyes off Jesus, my guiding Light on the straight and narrow path. I was on my way to a beautiful port, but not the one that God had prepared for me.

That was our first and last "real" date because he entered the Marines immediately afterward. Twelve weeks later Raul's parents invited me to go with them to his graduation from boot camp. I loved him even more as a Marine than I had when he was a civilian.

Raul's dad, Raul Christian Ries, was born in Mexico City. He was very kind and seemed to enjoy the fact that I was raised in Latin America and that I could speak to him in Spanish. Raul's mother, Josefina Fernandez, was a beautiful Spaniard woman who was born in New York and still spoke with the famous accent. She was tiny, jovial, and fun-loving. It was obvious that she loved her family very much and served them faithfully. She seemed to really like me for Raul. I liked her too. That day I also met Raul's brother and his two sisters, of whom he was very proud. His seven-year-old sister, Christina, and I bonded—for life! I felt right at home with Raul's family. They were Catholic, but they did not know God. I had no doubt, however, that they also could be saved.

I had a few other opportunities to spend time with Raul's family before he went to Vietnam. I was delighted by them and by their Latin culture. I told my parents how special Raul's family was. And they, seeing my determination to pursue Raul, began to pray more earnestly for their salvation as well. What I didn't tell them was that I had observed that Papy, Raul's dad, was an alcoholic, and that I'd noticed how troubled his mother was because of it. What Raul didn't tell me was that he'd been in a terrible and bloody fight and had been ordered by the court to either go to jail or go to Vietnam. We were both keeping secrets, but not from God.

I was taught from childhood that being unequally united with a non-believer leads to misery and grave consequences (2 Corinthians 6:14–16). However, I had decided to do things my way instead of God's way. I would disobey God, be united to a non-believer, take him to church, and be in disobedience to God, again. Raul was now my "first love." I never stopped going to church, but I was convicted continuously. My pastor, my church, my grandparents, Shirley, and my parents were all praying that I would repent. Instead, I busied myself with college, work, and church. Raul and I fell even more in love through our letters to each other. He continually pressed for marriage and I wrote him lengthy letters explaining the road to salvation. He promised that he would become whatever I wanted him to become. Yet there was no doubt in my mind that I would reap heavy consequences if I married him.

Raul was wounded twice and received two purple hearts for his service in Vietnam. Though his parents suffered greatly at the news, I never felt that he would die. After eleven months of heavy combat duty he was sent to the Oakland Naval Hospital in Monterey, California, where he was treated for "severe emotional trauma." Raul assured me that it was routine for soldiers to spend time at the hospital recuperating from the war. Now we could be together at last!

> I would, alone, suffer the consequences of my sin. But I trusted God to fix the mess I had made. I would marry Raul and show him the path to God.

Raul's family went to church with me that Easter in 1968. And I, in my disobedience, fell into sin that week and got pregnant. All my plans and dreams for the future were crushed. I was brokenhearted and repentant. Raul was thrilled. To him it meant a new life with a Christian wife and a baby. It was everything he wanted: an escape from twenty years in a verbally and physically abusive home—an escape from his life.

I didn't tell my parents. I would, alone, suffer the consequences of my sin. But I trusted God to fix the mess I had made. I would marry Raul and show him the path to God. Because of my sudden change in plans, my mother figured out that I was pregnant. She and Daddy demonstrated their unconditional love for me by giving us a wonderful ceremony. I was grateful. My daddy gave me away, and he and my pastor married us. No one but God knew the shame that I felt as I walked up the aisle arm-in-arm with my daddy. During the ceremony Raul was distracted admiring me, so I said my vows to the Lord. But as Raul and I walked back down the aisle together, I was suddenly enveloped with warmth, light, and unspeakable joy. I sensed God's grace, the unmerited favor that He bestows on sinners.

Six months later our beautiful son, Raul Junior, was born, and fourteen months after that I gave birth to our sweet son, Shane. The boys brought tenderness into our marriage. Raul enrolled in college and worked very hard providing for our family. However, he didn't seem to know how to communicate without being angry. Day by day he grew increasingly verbally and physically abusive. I had never been abused in any way. My parents never demeaned me or called me filthy names. They called me Sharon or "Darling." My mother never raised her voice to me. Over the years, I have learned what abuse is: to ignore, reject, continuously demean, falsely accuse, pursue, control, and cast out. It is to physically hurt a person; to seek to wound a person emotionally and destroy the character of one who is created in God's image and for His purpose. The abuser will ultimately destroy himself and his loved ones. God can heal the abuser if he simply repents and asks the Lord for His divine love. God is able to set free those who are bound by this destructive sin.

I often wept bitterly in those days—for my sins, because of the abuse, and for what could have been if only I had stayed on the path of obedience. I began despairing as the psalmist describes in Psalm 77. One day as I lay in my bed, Jesus penetrated my darkness. He said, "I am the Light and the Life." I drew back the curtains and stood in the light coming through the window and repented of my unbelief. I again surrendered my heart to God, His Word, and His will for me. This time, I would follow Jesus closely. I spent my days raising my little boys in the ways of the Lord and daily praying for them. I sang the "old" hymns and wrote love letters and poems to Jesus that flowed from my Bible reading. I decided to fight for my family. My rebellion had brought us all misery and shame, but now, through the guidance of God's Word, I would lead them to a life of victory (2 Corinthians 10:4).

After four years, I became physically weary and emotionally sorrowful because of Raul's constant abuse. I also grew increasingly concerned that the boys would grow up to be like him. God commands parents to train up their children in the ways of the Lord (Proverbs 22:6). Our boys were full of life and loved Jesus, but they were witnessing anger and abuse on a daily basis. After much prayer and soul searching, I began thinking that I should get away from Raul so that I could shield the boys from him. I would finish my education at Bethany Bible College in Santa Cruz, California, and raise them in a Christian environment.

The Jesus Movement was in full swing at the time. Hippies were meeting in a tent in Santa Ana, California, and were getting saved by the thousands. It was an incredible movement of the Holy Spirit. For some time, Mother had been encouraging us to go to the church in Santa Ana, but Raul was not interested.

I was attending Sunday school at the Assemblies of God church in the city of Covina, and sometimes I could get Raul to go with me. On Sunday, April 15, 1972, Raulie, Shano, and I were in church, and during the Sunday night altar call, I saw Raul storm down the left aisle toward the altar. I thought it was blasphemous for him to be pursuing after me during prayer. Fearing what he could be up to, I rushed home and locked myself in our house. Before long, he was beating on the front door and yelling, "Open the door! Open the door!" I did as he asked, knowing that he would knock the door down if I didn't. But I accidentally left the security chain on. He peeked through the opening, and with a big smile, said, "I'm born again!" I slammed the door in his face. *He's gone crazy*, I thought, but out of fear I opened the door. He said, "Sharon, I'm really born again. I love you. I'm sorry for all that I have done to you and the boys. . . . We are going to be happy." He explained, "There was a guy on TV with a lot of hippies talking about how God had changed their lives and I began to cry. I haven't cried since I was little. . . . I asked Jesus to change me, and Sharon, He did. I am forgiven! . . . I am not the same!"

Raul had experienced the miraculous conversion for which I had long prayed. I was trying to believe him but I couldn't. He tried to kiss me. I told him not to touch me. His mouth and his hands had hurt me, and I didn't want him or his hands close to my face. I didn't trust him anymore and I didn't want to forgive him. I thought, *What if he was faking his conversion so that I wouldn't leave him?*

Raul immediately began telling everybody about the miracle of his conversion. He called our family and friends. At first his parents were very upset, but eventually his entire family got saved, including his grandparents. He immediately invited everybody to go to Sunday school with us and won a plate for bringing the most people to church. He then loaded up our big, red Dodge van with anyone who would go, and took us to "the tent" in Santa Ana where the hippies were finding God through the preaching of young men who were being taught the Word in the ministry of a loving and tender shepherd, Pastor Chuck Smith. We learned that he was "the guy on TV" the day Raul had surrendered his life to Jesus. Pastor Chuck and the born-again hippies were being interviewed that day by the renowned evangelist Kathryn Kuhlman. (Coincidentally, I had made a decision for godliness at one of her evangelistic meetings when I was a young teen.)

Seeing that God was using Raul, I desperately asked Him to work in my life also. But I still had not truly forgiven Raul. One day we were visiting Raul's mother and I took an interest in a baseball photo of Raul when he was about ten years old. He looked so cute and innocent. The Lord gripped my heart with this thought: *He's My little boy; will you love him for Me?* I silently wept and repented. God's divine love poured into my soul and my hardened heart began to melt. My heavenly Father was Raul's loving Father too.

As Raul passionately shared his testimony and what he was learning from the Word of God, hundreds of people were being saved at his Kung Fu studio and at Baldwin Park High School where he was given permission to teach the Bible during the lunch break. There was no doubt that God had empowered Raul by His Holy Spirit to preach the gospel to the lost. I was in awe of God! Our fellowship of believers became Calvary Chapel of West Covina in 1974, and Pastor Chuck invited Raul to attend the first ministry school at Calvary Chapel of Costa Mesa.

Chuck's loving wife, Kay, poured out her heart as she taught and lived the "wholly devoted life" before all of us new pastors' wives. Over the years she has constantly exhorted us to live a holy life that is pleasing to the Lord. "We must live our lives with eternity in view," she tenderly reminds us. Her messages have kept me on the straight and narrow road and her life has impacted me for eternity.

Calvary Chapel was a place for the lost. Everyone worshiped in spirit and in truth before the Bible study began. Pastor Chuck taught through the Word of God, line upon line, week after week, and year after year! He taught God's truths in a language that everyone could understand. It ministered healing to my soul. Raul and I often attended "afterglows" [10] to pray and seek the Spirit's healing and guidance for our lives.

However, I still had a deep wound that refused to heal. It disturbed me greatly that Raul had hurt me so deeply and had not been punished for his deeds, nor suffered any consequences. He was spiritually free but I wasn't. As I questioned the Lord about this, a deeper revelation came to me about the sacrifice that Jesus had made on the cross. Jesus plainly said to me through His Word, "I was punished for his sins" (see Isaiah 53:5). *And mine*, I thought. I finally understood what it meant to "cherish the cross." I was to cling to the crucified One! God gave me a divine love for Raul that has endured the vicious assaults of Satan upon our lives. He then blessed our marriage with another child, our precious son, Ryan.

The Lord has given me the desires of my heart—a loving family and hundreds of godly friends. And, I get to serve Him every day of my life, joined by wonderful men and women worldwide who have been called by God. He fulfilled my childhood plea and sends me to the "uttermost parts of the earth" in search of lost souls. I thank God for those "light bearers" who, carrying their crosses, have illuminated the path that Raul and I, our children, and all of our grandchildren are to follow. That well-trodden path, wedged by the pilgrims of old, that is sprinkled with the blood of Jesus who gave His life for the world. My heart rejoices in God my Savior. Holy is His name!

Biography

Sharon Faith Ries is the wife of Raul Ries, senior pastor of Calvary Chapel Golden Springs in Diamond Bar, California. He is the evangelist of the Somebody Loves You Crusades and the Bible teacher of the *Somebody Loves You* radio program, which is heard daily throughout the United States and New Zealand. The story of Raul's miraculous conversion was recorded in Sharon's book, *My Husband, My Maker*, and in his book and movie, *From Fury to Freedom*, which has been distributed in several languages worldwide.

Sharon leads the women's ministries at Calvary Chapel Golden Springs, and does extensive missionary work throughout South America. Sharon has an intense passion to see souls saved in the uttermost parts of the world. She and Raul have three sons, a daughter-in-law, and two granddaughters.

Carol Wild

England's Child

"I, even I, am He who blots out your transgressions
for My own sake; and I will not remember your sins."
Isaiah 43:25

Isaiah 9:2 says, *The people who walked in darkness have seen a great light;*
those who dwelt in the land of the shadow of death, upon them a light has
shined. This is what happened to me: Once I walked in darkness, but now
I have seen the Light—I have seen Jesus! I gave my life to the Lord on July
29, 1968, in Pastor George Yeomans' office in a college of evangelism in
Kirkby-in-Ashfield, Nottinghamshire, England.

But maybe I should start a little further back. I grew up in Gateshead,
England. I was a coal miner's daughter, the eldest of two. My sister, Gloria,

is two years and nine months younger than me. We grew up in a relatively happy home. Our parents didn't go to church, but they never stopped us from going. From the age of six through age fourteen (until I discovered boys), I went to church. I loved to hear the stories of Jesus, and I said my prayers every night. I don't ever remember hearing that Jesus Christ died for me personally. My understanding was that He died on the cross for all of humanity. I lived my life thinking I was okay—I had a sense of right and wrong, but did things I knew were wrong. Even so, the Lord put many Christians in my path—from my Sunday school teachers to my gym teacher. I'm sure they were praying for me.

At the age of fifteen, the mine where my dad worked closed down, and he got another mining job in a town called Nottingham. Initially I thought it would be exciting to get to know a whole new set of friends, but my excitement was very short-lived. I soon felt the loneliness of leaving our extended family and I didn't particularly like Nottingham. After a few months we finally settled in and began to make a new life. My mom and I found work in the local factory and my sister attended a new school.

Several years went by and then one day a young red-headed man, who was the lead singer in a band, walked through my door. He had come to pick up my sister, as she was dating the band's lead guitarist. The red-head's name was Malcolm Wild (great name for a rock-and-roll singer). We began dating, and six months later, after asking my dad for my hand in marriage, he proposed.

Life was wonderful. I was twenty-one years old and Malcolm was twenty-two. We worked hard, saved hard, and bought our first home before our wedding. Six months after our engagement, on September 2, 1967, we were married in our parish church.

My sister married Alwyn Wall (the lead guitarist) six months later and they lived down the street from us. The four of us were best friends and did everything together. We were all Beatles fans, so we went to their concert in Sheffield and were obsessed with everything they did. George

Harrison had begun to get into transcendental meditation and we wanted to find out more about it. So off the four of us went to London. We met Paul McCartney and George Harrison, who actually gave us a contact in Nottingham to help us get initiated into meditation. We all knew there was more to life than what we were experiencing and we were searching to find the meaning of life. *Why not give meditation a try?* we thought, hoping it would be the answer. During our initiation we were each given a "secret" mantra and warned that it wouldn't work if we told it to anyone. The secrecy made it feel important. (Years later we compared our individual mantras and discovered they were all the same!) The four of us would sit around talking about how we felt. We all thought we were getting more peaceful, but instead we found ourselves getting frustrated at the smallest things—like birds interrupting our meditations in the mornings!

About this same time, a coworker of Malcolm's (his name was Howard) often brought his Bible into the lunchroom of the factory where they worked. One day Malcolm asked Howard if he believed what he was reading in the Bible, and they struck up a conversation. It was the first of many conversations that Malcolm would come home and tell me about. He was really interested in what Howard had to say about the Bible. But we had been initiated into transcendental meditation only a few months earlier and I wasn't ready to go back and revisit all the things I had heard from the Bible as a child.

Additionally, we had not yet been married one year and I was totally absorbed with decorating our brand-new house. One day when we were busy working on the house, Malcolm asked me if I would go with him to church the following Sunday. I don't know what got into me, but I said yes! Howard had suggested that we check out the church in our town. He said we would hear the gospel, which he insisted was the answer to all of life's questions. He also said someone would invite us to tea after the service. We found out later that Howard didn't know the people at this church. He had gone home and told his wife, "We must pray that someone will invite them to tea."

Malcolm and I went to the Sunday evening service and there happened to be a guest speaker that night, Pastor George Yeomans. His message went right over my head, but I could tell that the people in the congregation really believed that Jesus was alive. After his sermon, Pastor Yeomans stood at the door and shook hands with each person who left the church. When he greeted Malcolm and me, he asked if we were Christians. (He prob-

> When Pastor Yeomans began to talk about sin, I became very uncomfortable. I felt like he could see right through my sinful heart. . . . I blurted out, "Look, I'm not a sinner and I didn't want to come here."

ably suspected we weren't because I was dressed in a miniskirt with a big floppy hat, and my face was plastered in makeup!) I was the first to speak up and answered, "Oh, yes!" "When did you become Christians?" he asked. "Oh, tonight," I said, not having a clue what he was talking about.

He ushered us into a little room and began to share the gospel with us. His secretary was there also and both of them were so excited to talk about what Jesus had done in their lives. When Pastor Yeomans began to talk about sin, I became very uncomfortable. I felt like he could see right through my sinful heart. It was as if all the bad things I had done were visible to him. I didn't know it at the time, but I was feeling the conviction of the Holy Spirit. So I blurted out, "Look, I'm not a sinner and I didn't want to come here. It was my husband's idea." Then I turned my back on them.

Pastor Yeomans was a wise man. He could see that I was resistant and decided to invite us to come to his college of evangelism for tea the next day. (God answered the prayer of Howard and his wife, Doreen!) I thought, *Great! Let's say yes and get out of here quick.* Malcolm did say yes and got directions, but I was still thinking, *No way!* However, on the way home we both said, "Boy, it was all about Jesus in there."

I had no intention of going to tea. As we resumed our decorating the next day, the subject of tea with the pastor never came up. I remember thinking, *Great! Malc has forgotten.* But then, at about 3:30 p.m., he said, "Are you going to get ready, Luv, to go to tea?" My first thought was, *Oh no!* And then I decided, *Well, I'll show this Pastor Yeomans. I won't get dressed up and I won't put on any makeup* [like he cared]! *And I'll ask him some tough questions: "If God is so good, why did He allow so many innocent children to die in Wales in a tragic mud slide last year?" And, "Why do so many bad things happen to good people?"* Not very original, but I thought I would really stump him. Another question I had grappled with from childhood was, *Why did Jesus cry, "My God, My God, why have You forsaken Me,"* from the cross? I never could understand how God could have turned His back on Jesus. I was going to ask him that one too!

With those thoughts, I set off for tea. When we arrived, there were a lot of young people walking around. Everyone seemed so friendly. We were taken into a large study with huge stuffed chairs that made us feel right at home. The fire was blazing in the fireplace and we made some small talk until the tea tray was brought in. We began to talk about the Bible, the Gospels, and Jesus's death on the cross. I never asked any of my questions *because* they were all being answered by the things Pastor Yeomans was saying.

Everything suddenly began to make sense. He said that Jesus had died *for me personally* on the cross, and that even if I had been the only person in the world He would still have died. Then he explained that my sin was placed upon Jesus when He cried, *My God, My God, why have You forsaken Me?* Jesus had taken my sin upon Himself, and the Father, who is a holy God, could not look at sin. Well, there it was.

The Light broke through and I could see it all so clearly. I knew I was a sinner in need of a Savior. I couldn't wait. I interrupted the conversation and said, "Okay, what do I have to do to get saved! I want to give Jesus my heart; I believe He died for me and my sins when He hung on the cross." Pastor Yeomans smiled, looked at Malcolm, and said, "What about you? Do you want to give your heart to the Lord?" Malcolm's answer was, "Well, if Jesus is who He says He is, then yes I do!" We knelt down on the floor right then and there and prayed. I felt very embarrassed. I had never prayed out loud in front of Malcolm or anyone else. We asked the Lord to forgive us and to come into our lives.

After we got up from our knees, Pastor Yeomans said we must write this date down because, like our wedding day, July 29, 1968, would be a day to remember. And then he called a married couple into his office and asked us to go with them. I went with the woman and Malc went with the man. The woman explained what had happened to me. She said I had been born again and that I was a new creation (Romans 8:9; 2 Corinthians 5:17). She told me that the Lord had wiped away my sins. It was like He had buried them in the deepest part of the ocean and then put up a sign for the Devil that says *No Fishing*! She said, "Whenever he comes — *and he will* — and he says to you, 'Well, you didn't ask Him to forgive this one, or you forgot to think about that one when you prayed,' remember your sins are gone, forever, and God will never remember them again." I didn't realize at the time that she was quoting Scripture, but as I began reading the Word for myself, I came across these verses:

> Isaiah 43:25: I, even I, am He who blots out your transgressions for My own sake; *and I will not remember your sins.*

> Psalm 103:12: *As far as the east is from the west,* so far has He removed our transgressions from us.

> Jeremiah 31:34: For I *will forgive their iniquity, and their sin I will remember no more.*

She also told me that the Lord would always be with me; He now lived inside me:

Matthew 28:20: *"Teaching them to observe all things that I have commanded you; and lo, I am with you always, even to the end of the age."* Amen.

John 14:17: "The Spirit of truth, whom the world cannot receive, because it neither sees Him nor knows Him; but you know Him, for He dwells *with you* and will *be in you.*"

Wow, did I feel clean! As we drove home I told Malcolm that if I died right then, I knew I would be going to heaven. Someone had said that I had given my life to Jesus, and therefore my name was written in the "Lamb's Book of Life." I imagined the Lord with a pen in His hand writing my name in this big book. I pictured red ink flowing from the pen as He wrote, and the ink was His blood (Revelation 3:5, 21:27). The truths this woman shared with me that night helped me so much in my early walk with the Lord. She also said that I should tell someone what had happened to me (Matthew 10:32).

Malcolm and I couldn't wait to tell my sister and her husband that we had found the answer to all our searching. We went to see them the next night. Malc went into the woods with Alwyn and I sat with my sister, Gloria. It was hard to know where to begin. I think I blurted out, "I have some wonderful news to tell you. I have become a Christian. I gave my life to Jesus Christ, and He has written my name in His Lamb's Book of Life!" She wasn't impressed. She said, "What! The Lamb's Book of Life? What's that?" After we had talked for a while and Malcolm and Alwyn came back, they agreed to go to church with us the next night. After hearing the gospel, they both gave their lives to the Lord. That was thirty-six years ago.

My life took on new meaning and my appetite for spiritual things seemed unquenchable. My parents were next on the list of people with whom we shared the good news. To my surprise my mom told me I had become a Christian after I had been christened as a baby. This confused me so I asked Pastor Yeomans about it. He told me to ask her where in the Bible it says I had to be christened to become a Christian. Of course she couldn't answer that question, so I realized the Bible doesn't teach that at all. It was very hard trying to convince my parents of their need for Jesus, but I kept on sharing with them whenever we were together.

Our first baby boy, Joel, was born a couple of years after we were saved. Nineteen months later our daughter, Rachel, arrived. During these years Malcolm and Alwyn had begun to write songs about Jesus and what He had done in their lives. Pretty soon every Christian coffee house in England was asking them to perform their songs. It became increasingly difficult for them to hold down their day jobs and continue with their growing music ministry. During this time our second son, Julian, was born. When he was only a few months old, Malcolm and Alwyn went full-time into the music ministry.

My life became very difficult. At times, I felt like I was raising our three children by myself. I was jealous of Malcolm's freedom, his travel experiences, and the impact he was having on people's lives for Jesus. It seemed so unfair that he got to lead what seemed like an exciting life while I had to stay at home with the children. I would go into bad moods just before he left and say awful things like, "Don't worry about us. We'll be fine, *although we don't have any money.* I'll take the children down to Mom's; she'll feed us. Have a great time. See you when you get back." Once he was gone, I would go before the Lord and say how sorry I was. I would beg Him to get Malcolm to call so I could apologize. I was angry and frustrated at how my life was turning out, so I began to complain to the Lord about it.

One night after the children were in bed I was gazing out the window at the falling snow, and I started to think about what life would be like if Malcolm had a bad accident on the motorway and died. I thought of other scenarios too. For example, I wondered what would happen if a young girl flashed her eyes at him during a concert and he fell in love with her and didn't come back to us. I didn't know it at the time, but looking back, I see how the Lord was getting my attention. He showed me that no matter what happened to Malcolm, I would still have a relationship with Him. I began to realize that Malcolm was my first love and that the Lord needed to become my first love. And so He began very gently to reveal what He was doing. God had allowed all these absences so that I would turn to Him and develop my own deep relationship with Him. I had often thought about the day when I would stand before the Lord. I would always envision myself standing at Malcolm's side and I would say, "I'm Carol, Malcolm's wife." I began to realize that I would have to stand alone before God.

And so began my schooling with just Jesus and me. He began to teach me how to grow in Him no matter what happened in my circumstances. I had thought that being left behind with the children was punishment for some terrible thing I had done in my life, but in those long evenings after they were tucked up in their beds, I began to see that I didn't have to go traveling around the country to minister to others or see people come to know Jesus. I had been too caught up in myself! The Lord said to me, "Here is your ministry! Here they are, right in your home!" I remember thinking, *Oh wow! Thank You Lord for my own little ministry; I can teach the children to love and serve You right here at home.* I asked God to make me the best mom for them and the best wife for Malcolm. I asked Him to help me to love Malcolm and to send him off to minister with my blessing and prayers. I cried a lot during those evenings alone with Jesus. They were the most difficult of times and the best of times. People would say, "Oh, make the most of these times while your children are small, because before you know it they will be all grown up." I would think, *Yeah, right!* But they were right! (Now I am the grandmother of five grandchildren and I love it!)

I had never told Malcolm how I was feeling, maybe because I knew it was selfish. However, one day when we were talking, it came out that I was envious of the times he toured with people like Billy Graham and Billy Strachan (a well-known Scottish teacher and principal of Capernwray Bible College, who traveled with Billy Graham on his Spree '73 tour). I don't know how he came to know so much more about the Scriptures than I did since we came to Christ together, but he shared with me from 1 Samuel 30:21–24. This passage says that those who stay home and "look after the stuff" share in the rewards gained by those who go into battle. Knowing that I would share in the eternal rewards of Malcolm's ministry had a profound effect upon my life; I never looked at ministry the same way again. My circumstances didn't change, but my attitude changed and I was able to enjoy my life.

I lived on the corner of a busy street and got to meet a lot of women my own age. They too were just starting their families. I would share the Lord with my new friends and invite them to church. Gloria and Alwyn lived close by and between us we had five children. My life was consumed with raising up the children. Taking them to church was especially difficult when Malcolm was away. Many times I would not want to get everyone dressed and off to church, but I knew Malcolm would call me from the road and ask me about it, and I couldn't face telling him I hadn't gone. I was always glad I made the effort because I really enjoyed the fellowship. I never got much out of the sermons, as there were no classes for the children, and I had to keep all three of them occupied during the service. That was a challenge every week! But I was growing, even if I didn't see it. I would prop my Bible on the side of my chair while I was feeding our youngest child, and I guess a little Bible reading was better than none at all.

The Lord began to provide for our family in ways I had never experienced before. One time when we had no money and were beginning to get worried about how we were going to pay our water bill, the postman dropped a letter through the door. When I opened it, I found the amount of money needed to pay the bill. Malcolm and I both cried!

And then, after nine years of traveling, Alwyn decided it was time for him to stay home and go back to work at the factory where he had previously worked. This meant the end of the band, and for us it was a very difficult time. It was especially hard for Malcolm as he searched for God's will. However, not long after Alwyn's decision, the Lord opened a door for us to go south, to a place called Shaftesbury, Dorset, to work with a friend who had a burden for the young people there. The move meant packing up, putting our house on the market, and leaving our parents. The decision was easy and difficult all at the same time. I was ready because of the work the Lord had been doing in my life. I had been so into possessions, and yet, about a week before this opportunity arose, I had turned to Malcolm and said, "I could leave all this stuff behind; it really doesn't have any hold on me."

I couldn't believe it was so easy for me to leave our first home. I felt like we were about to start on a wonderful journey that the Lord had ordained for us. It was a brand-new beginning. The Lord provided a new home for us through friends who were selling one that was empty. Moving day came and the driver of our moving van happened to be a Christian. As we were driving, he asked me how many rooms were in our new house. I had no idea! I had never even seen it. He was shocked and I think a little worried for us. The drive took about six hours, and as we pulled up to the house, the shock on this man's face was something one sees in the movies. He shouted at the top of his lungs, "Praise the Lord! Halleluiah! I have never seen such a beautiful 'faith house' in all my life." He said he had been getting very nervous for us as we were nearing our destination. He had driven others to "faith destinations," and all of them had been huge disappointments. He was so excited! Yes, indeed, what we beheld was a sight for sore eyes! It was a beautiful detached house with rooms to spare, and there were lovely gardens and an orchard at the back. We got out of the van and joined hands in thanksgiving to the Lord for a beautiful faith house.

Joel and Rachel went to the nearby school and Julian and I filled our days picking and freezing the fruit. When our home sold, we began looking for something to buy in Shaftesbury, but the Lord never once opened that door. Then we heard the house we were living in had been sold. We had to be out by March 31, 1977. We didn't have any idea where we would go, but Malcolm was scheduled to be in California for a musician's retreat organized by Maranatha! Music, so he left.

I carried on with the jobs at hand: looking through real estate advertisements, cleaning house, and taking care of the children. He had been gone about a week when he called to tell me he had been offered a job with Maranatha! Music. He asked me to pray and said he would call back in a day or so. I was in the children's bedroom, cleaning and looking out the windows, thinking what a lovely view it was, when all of a sudden my mind was filled with the words, *Trust and obey*. At first I thought it was a song that was going through my mind, and I started to sing, but then I suddenly felt that it was the Lord speaking to me. Those words had come out of the clear blue sky: *Trust and obey*. I asked the Lord, "Is this You, Lord, speaking to me? Do You want me to trust and obey You in this matter? Do You want us to walk through this door You have opened?" I sensed that, yes, this opportunity was from the Lord—I just knew it.

We actually flew to California on March 31, 1977—the very day we had to be out of our house. It was amazing to be on our way to a new country with three children when we really didn't know what was waiting for us there. I had some concerns, but the Scripture says *God is able to do exceedingly abundantly above all that we ask or think* (Ephesians 3:20), and that is exactly what He did! I was concerned about the schools for the children, but Calvary Chapel of Costa Mesa had its own Christian school, Maranatha Christian Academy. I thanked the Lord hundreds of times for that wonderful school. A house had already been rented for us and was waiting when we arrived. The Lord knew our needs and provided for them in every way.

Our lives took a completely different direction after we moved to California. Malcolm was home more often. We lived across the street from the church, and I couldn't get enough of the teaching there. I had never heard the Word taught the way it was taught at Calvary Chapel. And I was amazed at the number of people who attended—there were three services on Sunday mornings! I had never seen anything like that in England. I thought everyone in America must be a Christian.

I loved to go to Kay Smith's women's Bible study on Friday mornings and will be forever grateful for the practical truths she taught me from the Word. Sometimes, though, I felt lonely. I would see all these women leave together in groups for lunch or to play tennis after the study was over, and I would pray for the Lord to bring a godly woman into my life—a best friend from whose life I could glean. My desire was for an older woman who would help me to become a good wife, mother, and Christian. After praying for what seemed a lifetime, I was once again asking the Lord to send me a friend one Friday morning as I walked home from the study. Suddenly I was struck with the thought that He had already put a godly woman in my life! (I believe this thought was from Him.) It was Kay Smith. She was teaching me from the Word how to please the Lord and I was gleaning from her. I never asked God for a best friend again!

We were living the dream life for an English Christian family, with our kids in Christian school and a great church across the road. Malcolm used to say, "I'm sure someone in England is selling our address as free room and board for Christians wanting to see what is happening in California." We were in the middle of a wonderful work of God's Spirit known as the Jesus Movement, and our house was always open to the many English folk who wanted to see firsthand what was happening. After a time, Malcolm was asked to become an assistant pastor. At first this seemed very strange, as our thoughts had never really gone any further than the music ministry, but God was working in a way that we had never even imagined.

After seven-and-a-half years at Calvary Chapel of Costa Mesa, where we grew in God's Word and witnessed many strange and wonderful works of the Lord, He opened a door for us to move to Florida. Malcolm went first to meet the group of people who were looking for a pastor. After meeting with them he wanted me to fly out to see what I thought. One night I was sitting alone in the hotel room while Malcolm was with the elders praying for guidance. I asked the Lord to show me from His Word if this is what He wanted our family to do. I waited a long time just reading and praying. He led me to Ephesians chapter 2. I started reading and in verse 20 it said, *Jesus Christ Himself being the chief cornerstone.* The church was called Cornerstone! I was taken aback and asked the Lord, "Please, would You confirm this to me through Your Word?" Not long after I turned to 1 Peter, and there in chapter 2 verse 6 were the words, *Behold, I lay in Zion a chief cornerstone!* I closed the Word and felt this was indeed the Lord speaking to my heart. I didn't know at the time how important this Word from the Lord would be.

A few months later we moved into another house that I had not seen; the realtor had picked it out for our family. We lived there for a couple years and then I actually got to plan and build our own home. We can never out-give the Lord! Again He blessed us *exceedingly abundantly above all that we ask or think.*

Only six months after we had moved to Merritt Island, Florida, a difficult situation arose in the church that made me question whether we should stay or go back to California. When I said this to Malcolm, he turned to me and said, "What was it that the Lord showed you when you were praying about coming here?" I remembered the event in the hotel room and said, "We were supposed to come." Malcolm said, "If this situation is of the

Lord, then I don't want to get in the way. But if it's not, then the Lord will take care of it. Either way I know we are supposed to be here."

And we are still here in Merritt Island! The Lord continues to bless my life. I am still learning and growing and still waiting on Him to see what He has for the remaining years of our lives. Who knows where we may end up? Only the Lord knows, but as we walk in His will, He will be there with us!

Biography

Carol Wild is the wife of Malcolm Wild, senior pastor of Calvary Chapel of Merritt Island, Florida (the first Calvary Chapel in Florida). They have served there for over twenty years. Carol oversees the church's women's ministry, which includes a Bible study, a prayer chain, local retreats, and regional conferences. She has taught at Calvary Chapel women's retreats and conferences across the country and in England. Carol's heart is to minister to women whenever and wherever the Lord opens the door. She and Malcolm are the parents of three married children and have five grandchildren.

Epilogue

As you have read through these stories, perhaps they have made you consider your own spiritual need. It is our prayer and hope that the same extraordinary God who transformed our lives will not only redeem yours for all eternity, but that He will also restore your life here on earth—so that it abounds with new purpose and meaning.

The steps to a new life are simple:

1. Realize you are a sinner.
2. Turn from your sins and confess them to God.
3. Believe that Jesus paid the price for your sins when He died on the cross at Calvary.
4. By faith, receive the free gift of salvation.

We pray you won't wait a moment longer to be *Redeemed and Restored*!

My Story

You have read our stories, so now add your own story to this book of remembrance of the glorious things God has done.

Endnotes

1. Redman, Matt. "Befriended," Where Angels Fear to Tread. Kingsway Thank-you Music, 2001.

2. Moen, Don. "God Will Make a Way," God Will Make A Way. Integrity Music, 2003.

3. Tozer, A.W. *The Pursuit of God*. Grand Rapids: Fleming H. Revell Company, 1983.

4. "Jesus, Thou Joy of Loving Hearts" by St. Bernard of Clairvaux. Twelfth-century.

5. Sweeting, George. *Great Quotes and Illustrations*. Nashville: W Publishing Group, 1985.

6. Noonan, Peggy. *Life, Liberty, and the Pursuit of Happiness*. New York: Random House, 1984.

7. Lewis, C.S. *Mere Christianity*. New York: Touchstone, 1980.

8. "Great Is Thy Faithfulness." Words by Thomas O. Chisholm. Hope Publishing, 1923.

9. "The Old Rugged Cross." Words and music by George Bennard, 1913.

10. An "afterglow" is a prayer and worship service at which the gifts of the Spirit are fully exercised.